NOTES ON A SCANDAL

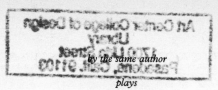

by the same author

plays

DEALER'S CHOICE

CLOSER

AFTER MISS JULIE

HOWARD KATZ

HOOP LANE

THE MUSICIANS

DON JUAN IN SOHO

screenplays

CLOSER

NOTES ON A SCANDAL

Patrick Marber

based on the novel by

ZOË HELLER

faber and faber

First published in 2006
by Faber and Faber Limited
3 Queen Square, London WC1N 3AU

Typeset by Country Setting, Kingsdown, Kent CT14 8ES
Printed in England by Mackays of Chatham plc, Chatham, Kent

Patrick Marber is hereby identified as author of this work
in accordance with Section 77 of the Copyright, Designs
and Patents Act 1988

A CIP record for this book
is available from the British Library

ISBN 978-0-571-23610-7
ISBN 0-571-23610-3

2 4 6 8 10 9 7 5 3 1

CONTENTS

NOTES ON THE SCREENPLAY

In the winter of 2003 my wife was in bed reading a novel. She was gurgling with delight: 'You've *got* to read this!' And then she refocused on the page, continuing to purr with pleasure.

A few days later a package arrived from the producer, Scott Rudin. By coincidence it was a copy of the same novel and a request to read it with a view to adapting it for the screen.

Whenever I'm sent a book one of my first thoughts is, 'If I take this on I'm going to have to read it at least ten times. So how do I feel about that?' When I reached the end of *Notes on a Scandal*, I turned immediately to the first page to read it all again. I was staggered by its brilliance. How had Zoë Heller done it? How had the narrator crept up on me with such stealth? Why hadn't I detected how loopy she was? How had the author achieved such a rich brew of comedy, creepiness, satire and suspense? And why had it moved me so much?

I knew I wanted to write the screenplay but the prospect was intimidating: I loved the novel, but knew that to be faithful to its spirit I might have to betray some of its 'moves'. (I suspect all screenwriters who adapt from other sources know this feeling.) And the setting was a sort of drizzly London I knew only too well – a few miles up the road from our flat. And the story was all about lonely, desperate people in shabby rooms. My wife allayed my fears by pointing out that this was my natural subject – if not my natural habitat.

A second pressure was that Judi Dench and Cate Blanchett had both read and loved the novel and expressed keen interest in doing the screen version of it. To pull off a film of *Notes on a Scandal* was always going to require two incredible actors. And here were two supreme ones waiting to read what I wrote. I've written scripts with actors in mind and I've written scripts with no idea of who might play the roles. This one began to feel like a mission; the deeper I got into it the more I sensed that with these two extraordinary actors playing the leads we might make something great. The more I wrote, the more enticing the prospect became; it *had* to be them!

In the novel Barbara narrates the story from the perspective of a journal she's keeping, her 'Notes on the Scandal'. My instinct was to replicate this by using voice-over. The current orthodoxy seems to be that 'VO' is a copout: 'too literary', not 'cinematic'. But many of my favourite films use it: *All About Eve*, *Taxi Driver*, *Manhattan*, to name but three, and all are brilliantly written. So I decided to embrace 'VO'. It enabled me to thread Barbara's insistent voice throughout the film. And, crucially, it became the means by which the film could reveal her alarming self-delusion. These choices, which now seem so obvious, took me eight or nine drafts to arrive at. As the screenplay progressed I realised that the VO needed to push even further so that the disparity between what Barbara says and what she *is* becomes ever more disturbing. Consequently, the whole climax of the film became Sheba's discovery of the source of the voice-over, namely, Barbara's diary. And I decided that once the diary is 'exposed' the voice-over would cease. I'm now a shameless fan of VO. It became, for me, the engine of the whole screenplay.

Another big decision I had to make was when to reveal the key piece of information: that Sheba is having an affair with a fifteen-year-old boy. In the novel we're told of this 'scandal' from the off, it's the 'given' of the story. I decided to hold off this revelation and give the film a different shape. I structured it as per the manual, in three acts. The first act climaxes with Barbara discovering the affair, the second with 'the world' discovering it, and the third deals with the fallout and discovery of the diary. In short, three acts exposing three secrets.

There was another problem to solve: should Barbara know more, or less, or the same as the audience? Whereas in the book she's omniscient, I realised (after months of trial and error) that on film I might be able to play with this. Thus she could be the holder of information for a period of the film and then be in the dark and then continue to know and 'not know' throughout. This would help generate the 'suspense' element of the novel, the flow and control of information being central to it. At the beginning Barbara's our guide, a seemingly reliable guardian of the truth. We discover everything through her, and then, once we've got to know her, the film and Sheba 'betray' her. This is marked with a shift in the film's point of view. It's prefigured in the pub scene when Barbara commands Sheba to tell her all. The film goes into a flashback sequence in which Sheba narrates her account of events leading up to the affair. This is the first time we've seen things from an angle distinct from Barbara's, the first time we see Sheba from an 'objective' point of view. We begin to realise that Barbara's version of Sheba is madly different from the reality. The whole story is contained in that divergence.

The full shift in perspective occurs a scene later, just after Barbara and Sheba hug goodbye. Instead of the camera following Barbara (as it has done for forty minutes) it now goes with Sheba into her house, where Barbara is 'excluded'. The effect of this, I hope, is to balance the audience's interest in the two women. By giving them 'access' to Sheba at this moment and by suddenly allowing the audience to know more than Barbara, I tried to achieve formally what the screenplay was doing psychologically. The characters are engaged in an unspoken duel, they dance around each other throughout, neither of them declaring the truth until the bitter end.

I should add that this strange dance would not have been achievable without the particular qualities Judi and Cate have in abundance. They managed to make the characters sympathetic, entertaining and ferociously alive even at their worst. Both of them accepted this without question: they embraced the discomfort of it and played all the contradictory emotions simultaneously. They revealed the humanity beneath the desperation; it was thrilling to watch.

And then there was the ending. In the book Sheba becomes Barbara's prisoner. The older woman secures her prey – but at a price; the one she 'loves' is destroyed. It's great. But on film, after ninety minutes of cut and thrust, I worried it might seem a touch inconclusive. I took a view that a more cinematic resolution might be to push the two women apart. So I sent Sheba back to her husband (whom I made a little more genial than in the novel) and I gave Barbara a new friend to play with. The cumulative effect, I hope, is of two lives crashing into each other and then tearing apart. Sheba is burnished and can now go forward without artifice whereas Barbara is calcified and can never change.

I think this is the thematic conclusion of the book too, if not its actual dramatic action. Thankfully, Zoë agreed, and liked the ending of the film. She was, in fact, a perfect 'adaptee': interested but not intrusive, curious but not covetous. As the daughter of one screenwriter and the wife of another, she perfectly understood that an element of benevolent piracy is involved in adaptation. She was an encouraging emailer and generous reader of my work in progress. If you haven't read her book, then please do – I can't recommend it highly enough, it's the glorious sow to this runt.

My thanks also to Scott Rudin for offering me the job and for greatly helping me to write this film. 'Helping' is inexact. He pummelled, coerced and occasionally caressed the words from me. His ideas were potent and his communication of them exact. Dramaturgy is something of a lost art. When a writer finds a producer who knows his onions it's a very great help. Mr Rudin is more than familiar with his onions.

I also thank the other producer of this film, Robert Fox. He was a brilliantly astute reader of the screenplay and of the film as it was being made. It was a pleasure to while away the long hours on set with him – laughing, kvetching, nipping off to the bookies and fighting over the last Mars bar at the craft table. His handling of the 'talent' is legendary; it was a pleasure being handled by Mr Fox.

Richard Eyre directed with his customary air of humorous misery. He would say – modestly – that he did nothing, just shot what I wrote. I would say – immodestly – that he had the good grace to do so. I'm very grateful he did it so beautifully. Having produced my first two plays at the National Theatre, Richard is one of the people responsible for making me a writer. Tempting though it may have been, he never once said, 'I created a monster' – at least, not to my face. I thank him for that and much else besides.

I don't want to bore on about how great Judi Dench is. If you've bought this book you've probably seen the film and know it already. Watching her rehearse a scene and then nail it on camera, to see her giving life to the words I'd written . . . well, that's about as good as it gets. The moment on the bench when she talks about her 'vision' of herself always moves me in ways I can't understand. Which is my favourite way to be moved.

And then Cate Blanchett, who seems to act with her nerve endings exposed. As with all great film actors, you feel as if she's showing you a fraction of what's inside her. I always love watching the scene in the summerhouse when Steven is wearing the hat she's made for her son. She seems to become sixteen again and then a distraught adult in the blink of an eye.

And Bill Nighy: sexy, hilarious, brilliantly broken, portraying fifteen years of lazy marital collapse with effortless economy. And then Phil Davis, immaculate as the hapless Brian in the longest scene in the film. And Andrew Simpson, given the tricky job of fancying Cate's 'Sheba', which he did with considerable aplomb.

There was also the pleasure of watching the great cinematographer Chris Menges at work. Ditto the masterful editors John Bloom and Antonia Van Drimmelen. And then hearing Philip Glass's score for the first time and being knocked out by it. And then there were Redmond Morris and Rachel Neale holding it all together and Tim Hatley and the Art Department were superb and the crew and the drivers too.

You get the point.

My thanks to everyone who made this film.

PM, October 2006

CAST AND CREW

Notes on a Scandal received its world premiere
in New York in December 2006

PRINCIPAL CAST
(*in alphabetical order*)

SASKIA	Alice Bird
SHEBA HART	Cate Blanchett
BRIAN	Phil Davis
BARBARA COVETT	Judi Dench
EMMA KENNEDY	Tameka Empson
BEN	Max Lewis
RICHARD HART	Bill Nighy
SUE HODGE	Joanna Scanlan
PETE	Philip Scott
STEVEN CONNELLY	Andrew Simpson
POLLY	Juno Temple

PRINCIPAL CREW

Producers	Scott Rudin
	Robert Fox
Executive Producer	Redmond Morris
Director	Richard Eyre
Original Music	Philip Glass
Cinematography	Chris Menges
Art Direction	Grant Armstrong
	Mark Raggett
Editors	John Bloom
	Antonia Van Drimmelen

Notes on a Scandal

Fade in:

EXT. PARLIAMENT HILL, NORTH LONDON – DAY (SEPTEMBER)

Barbara alone on a bench. She is high above the city; the view is magnificent.

She watches the couples, kids playing, families.

> BARBARA
> (*voice-over*)
> People have always trusted me with their secrets.

INT. SITTING ROOM – DAY

Barbara writing her diary in her one-bedroom basement flat.

> BARBARA
> (*voice-over*)
> But who do I trust with mine?

A whole shelf of hardback notebooks, her collection of diaries dating back to the 1950s.

> BARBARA
> (*voice-over*)
> You. Only you.

EXT. ARCHWAY ROAD – EARLY MORNING

The roar of traffic. The urban ravine of the Archway Road.

The red, black and gold cast-iron 'suicide bridge' which straddles it.

Barbara driving to work in her old VW Polo.

EXT. ST GEORGE'S SCHOOL/CAR PARK – MORNING

The school is a bleak Victorian building with various modern add-ons.

Barbara locks her car and heads for the main entrance.

INT. CLASSROOM – MINUTES LATER

Barbara takes out her lesson planner, text books, register. She organises them neatly on her desk.

Barbara stares at the rows of empty desks and chairs.

> BARBARA
> (*voice-over*)
> The first day of a new term.

Sound of Pupils arriving outside. Barbara observes them from her high window.

EXT. SCHOOL – DAY

Kids in school uniform stream through the gates.

> BARBARA
> (*voice-over*)
> Here come the local pubescent proles.

They play football, gossip, fight and skirmish. A diverse ethnic mix, about fifty per cent white.

> BARBARA
> (*voice-over*)
> The future shop assistants and plumbers. And doubtless the odd terrorist too.

A teacher (Brian) oversees the general activity.

Sheba Hart comes in through the main gates pushing her tatty old bicycle. She looks a little lost.

Brian directs her to the bike racks.

INT./EXT. RECEPTION AREA/MAIN COURTYARD – LATER

Barbara watches Ted Mawson (Deputy Head) outside with Sheba; he's introducing her to members of staff passing by.

BARBARA
(*voice-over*)
In the old days we confiscated cigarettes and 'wank mags'.
Now it's knives and crack cocaine. And they call it progress.

The school bell rings and Sheba is whisked away in another direction.

INT. CLASSROOM – ANOTHER DAY

Barbara writes WITTENBERG *on the board. Other stray phrases
already there:* DIET OF WORMS, MARTIN LUTHER.

She's teaching the Reformation to a class of bored sixteen-year-olds.

*The bell rings. The Pupils immediately snatch up their books to leave.
Barbara makes a gesture – they sit back down.*

KID
(*under his breath*)
Fuckin' poison granny.

Barbara surveys her class. Another gesture: 'You may go.'

INT. SPORTS HALL – AFTERNOON (A WEEK LATER)

*A committee meeting of around twenty Teachers, chaired by the
Headmaster, Sandy Pabblem.*

*His secretary (Gita) takes notes. The staff sit in chairs in a circle,
Barbara amongst them. In passing we see teachers Elaine Clifford and
Sue Hodge.*

PABBLEM
Before we start, can those of you who haven't delivered
your reports please lob 'em in my general direction.

*He goes round the circle. Staff hand him their school-issue report files,
all thick with their work.*

Thanks Bill, Elaine. Thank you, Linda – how's Greg?

LINDA
A bit better, thanks.

5

He holds his hands together – a gesture of emotional solidarity.

PABBLEM

Good, good.

Sheba comes in mouthing apologies for her lateness.

Ah! Has everyone met our new Art teacher, Sheba Hart?

General murmurs of 'Hello' and 'Welcome'.

I've invited Sheba to sit in on this meeting. As you know, I regard the arts as absolutely central to our policy of 'reform through nurture'.

Barbara gestures to the empty chair beside her. But another teacher (Bill Rumer) is comically commanding Sheba to sit next to him. Which she does.

Welcome to you.

Sheba takes out a note-pad and pen, looking nervous but keen. Pabblem continues collecting the reports.

Thank you, Sue. Ooh, that's a big one! I'll be up till the crack of dawn. Anyone else not handed in their homework?

He turns to Barbara, a hint of nervousness.

Barbara . . . ?

Barbara coolly produces her file. It's impossibly thin. Pabblem pretends to weigh it on his hand so that others can witness its paucity.

Encouraged by polite laughter, he opens it to reveal a single sheet of typed paper.

This is your report? On the History Department? On its entire workings? And your general thoughts for its future development?

BARBARA

You'll find it's quite thorough, Headmaster.

The teachers look tense but one or two are secretly amused – this is vintage Barbara. Gita looks appalled.

Pabblem stares at the report; it's one paragraph long.

> **PABBLEM**
> (*reads aloud*)
> 'The History Department functions much as one would
> expect for a school of this stature and intake. Examination
> results have been consistent for thirty years; below the
> national average but above the level of catastrophe.
> Recommendation: no change necessary.'

Barbara looks innocent, defying Pabblem to explode.

> **BARBARA**
> It took me most of the summer to write it.

He stares at her in impotent fury.

Barbara sneaks a look at Sheba.

> **BARBARA**
> (*voice-over*)
> Hard to read the wispy novice. Is she a sphinx or simply
> stupid?

EXT. PLAYGROUND – LUNCHTIME (A WEEK LATER)

*Sheba on playground duty, wrapped in a coat. She's patrolling
amongst the children. Barbara lurks nearby.*

> **BARBARA**
> (*voice-over*)
> Artfully dishevelled today. The tweedy tramp coat is an
> abhorrence. It seems to say, 'I'm just like you.' But clearly
> she is not.

Sheba intervenes between two kids sparring for a fight.

> **BARBARA**
> (*voice-over*)
> A fey person, I suspect. Fey.

*Suddenly – a roar from some Boys playing football. The goal scorer,
a Boy of fifteen, celebrates by whipping his shirt off and waving it in
jubilation – naked from the waist up.*

BARBARA

Put your shirt on!

BOY

I got the winner, Miss!

BARBARA

Glory be. Shirt.

Barbara glances at Sheba. She seems to be looking straight at her. Barbara wonders if Sheba disapproves of her ticking off the boy. As he runs away:

BARBARA

Good goal!

INT. SCHOOL CANTEEN – DAY

Barbara with her tray, eating lunch.

BARBARA
(*voice-over*)

She has certainly rippled the waters of our stagnant pond. They flock to her.

She watches Brian approaching Sheba.

BARBARA
(*voice-over*)

Even limp little Brian had a go. Oh, the horror.

Other Teachers, almost queuing for Sheba's attention.

INT./EXT. CANTEEN/COURTYARD – ANOTHER DAY

BARBARA
(*voice-over*)

And Fatty Hodge has pounced on her.

Barbara at a grubby canteen table – watching with a seemingly benign smile.

Sheba and Sue Hodge are on a bench outside, bathed in sunlight as they eat their sandwiches.

(*voice-over*)
A dubious double act: the blonde and the pig in knickers.

Sue chews like a rabbit as Sheba chortles.

INT. STAFF ROOM – A WEEK LATER

Barbara on a break. A few other Teachers dotted around. Brian comes in looking a little sheepish.

BRIAN
I just went past the Art Studio . . .

Barbara glances up.

It's bloody *Lord of the Flies* in there.

ELAINE
Have they gone for her?

BRIAN
(*nods*)
Torn her posters down, full-on paint fight, they're chanting, 'Get your tits out for the lads.' Girls too. It's carnage.

Barbara looks concerned, shares a shake of the head with Elaine. Bill looks up from the coffee station.

BILL
How was Madam?

BRIAN
Totally lost it. (*Imitates Sheba.*) 'Stop it! Stop it, you little fucking bastards.'

ELAINE
You should've stepped in.

Brian looks anxious, thinks she's right.

BILL
He didn't want to patronise the little lady. She'll be all right. The bourgeoisie need a good pasting now and then, reminds 'em where the true power resides.

He lobs a tea-bag in his mug.

This time next year she'll be Headmistress.

Antonia – another teacher – explodes:

> ANTONIA
> Oh Christ, will you shut up?! I'm trying to work!

She gestures to a mountain of school books she's marking.

> BILL
> (*sarcastic*)
> Sorry, sorry. Char, anyone? (*Pointedly.*) Babs?

> BARBARA
> Milk, no sugar.

> BILL
> Sweet enough?

> BARBARA
> Evidently.

> ELAINE
> Didn't her father invent inflation?

> BRIAN
> You what?

> ELAINE
> Wasn't her dad that academic; Donald whatsit? Economics bloke, he invented the word 'inflation'.

> BRIAN
> (*lying*)
> Oh yeah, yeah, I know who you mean.

> BARBARA
> I think you'll find that Mrs Hart's father was Professor Ronald Taylor. He didn't 'invent inflation', he devised a theory about the relationship between inflation and consumer expectation.

A silence. Brian and Elaine share a look at Barbara's expense.

INT. RECEPTION AREA – A WEEK LATER

The school day is over. Barbara walks through the lobby. She hears loud noises from the library and goes to look.

A photocopied sign on the door: HOMEWORK CLUB.

Through the window she sees two Boys fighting and Sheba desperately trying to separate them. Other Pupils encourage the fighters. It's mayhem.

> SHEBA
> Stop this immediately! Stop it both of you or you'll be up before the Head!

Barbara waits: let Sheba suffer or be her saviour?

The chaos continues – she takes a deep breath then bursts in, bellowing:

INT. LIBRARY – CONTINUOUS

> BARBARA
> ENOUGH!

Immediate silence. She parts the boys with swift and vigorous force. Sheba is hugely relieved, but Barbara's not finished yet.

> BARBARA
> (*to the Boys*)
> Outside. Now!

The two Boys file out. Barbara surveys the rest of the class. A Boy has a baseball cap on. Barbara points to her head, the Boy removes the cap from his own.

> BARBARA
> (*to other Kids*)
> Get on with your work!

Which they do, at once. And then Barbara marches out.

Sheba is unsure whether she's supposed to follow. Barbara gestures for her to come.

The boys are looking at the floor, hands in pockets.

> BARBARA
>
> Why were they fighting, Mrs Hart?

> SHEBA
>
> The motive was unclear.

> BARBARA
> *(to first Boy)*
>
> Davis I know – you're a little thug, aren't you? (*To second Boy.*) And who might you be?

The second boy is Steven Connolly (fifteen).

> STEVEN
> *(mumbling)*
>
> Steven Connolly, Miss.

> BARBARA
>
> What?

> STEVEN
>
> Steven Connolly, Miss.

> BARBARA
>
> Year?

> STEVEN
>
> Year Ten, Miss.

> BARBARA
> *(suddenly remembers)*
>
> The naked footballer. Why were you fighting? (*Beat.*) It's a perfectly simple question.

> STEVEN
>
> Dunno, Miss.

> BARBARA
>
> You don't know. One minute you're an inert lump, the next you're attempting to castrate a fellow pupil. Nothing occurred between these two states?

STEVEN

No, Miss.

BARBARA
(*cod Irish accent*)
Don't be a hero, Connolly, it's hardly da place. (*Pause.*) Yes?
Brain – mouth – and speak.

STEVEN
(*reluctantly*)
He was saying stuff about Miss. (*Nods at Sheba.*) He was
bang out of order.

This is news to Sheba.

BARBARA
(*to Davis*)
What did you say?

DAVIS

I never said nothing.

BARBARA
(*correcting him*)
'I didn't say anything'. (*To Connolly.*) What did he say? Oh,
come on!

CONNOLLY

He said she's a tart . . . he said he gave her one up the arse.

Sheba is shocked, Barbara is not.

BARBARA
(*to Davis*)
Did you indeed? Odious boy, apologise at once.

DAVIS
(*to Sheba*)
Sorry, Miss.

BARBARA

Deputy Head in the morning. Now back in, both of you.

The Boys shuffle into the library. Sheba shakes her head.

Little towers of testosterone, you'll get used to them.

SHEBA

Thank you so much. I'd better . . .

She gestures to the library but Barbara holds out her hand.

Oh, sorry, we haven't met properly, have we? Sheba Hart.
Art Department.

They shake hands.

BARBARA

Barbara Covett. History.

Barbara watches Sheba go back in. And smiles for the first time.

BARBARA
(*voice-over*)

Quite a nice voice, plummy and deep. As if her mouth was
pure, as if she'd never had a filling.

EXT. PLAYGROUND – ANOTHER DAY

Barbara and Sheba on playground duty. They smile at each other.

BARBARA
(*voice-over*)

The complexion of a white peach. One can almost see her
veins.

INT. SCHOOL CANTEEN – ANOTHER DAY

BARBARA
(*voice-over*)

Her trendy politics are similarly transparent.

Barbara, Sheba and Sue in the busy lunch queue.

BARBARA

We serve them best if we teach them to read, write and
add. They don't need to know about the basket-weavers of
Chile.

SUE

Barbara's very keen on the basics.

Sheba helps herself to some sad-looking coleslaw.

SHEBA
(*to Barbara*)
But when you started, didn't you want to give them a . . . a
real education? To help them overcome – well . . . (*sotto*) the
poverty of their backgrounds?

BARBARA
Yes of course but one soon learns that teaching is crowd
control – we're a branch of the social services.

Barbara spots a boy stealing a KitKat.

BARBARA
(*to boy*)
Put it back!

Sheba looks mournful, Sue tries to rally her.

SUE
Console yourself with the gems. Every now and then you
find one with an agile mind and a will to learn. That's when
it's satisfying, when you can really make a difference.

Sheba seems to really 'hear' this.

BARBARA
The rest is just cattle-prod and pray.

*They carry their trays to a vacant table. Barbara watches Sheba
intently: she seems so defeated by it all. But her sadness is beautiful to
behold . . .*

BARBARA
(*voice-over*)
I can see why others are beguiled by her.

EXT. ART STUDIO – LATE AFTERNOON (ANOTHER DAY)

Barbara waiting outside.

BARBARA
(*voice-over*)
But I wonder if she possesses the requisite heft?

Sheba emerges pulling on her coat, surprised to see Barbara there.

> BARBARA

Fancy a coffee?

> SHEBA

Mmm.

They head off. But then Barbara spots Sue emerging from the other side of the playground. She tries to usher Sheba at speed but Sue is gaining on them. A chase!

Fatally, Barbara glances back and Sheba follows suit. She sees the panting Sue and waits for her to join them – much to Barbara's frustration.

INT. GREASY CAFF – LATER

Barbara smoking – ever so slightly sulking. Sue and Sheba sip cappuccinos. Sue mock-taps the table with her spoon.

> SUE

Ahem. I've got a bit of an announcement.

> BARBARA

You're leaving St George's?

> SUE

No!

> BARBARA
> (*flatly*)

Oh, you're pregnant.

Sue registers a moment of anti-climactic sadness.

> SHEBA

That's fantastic! Congratulations! When are you due?

> SUE

June the seventh.

> SHEBA

A summer baby, how lovely.

BARBARA
(*suddenly perks up*)
So you'll be taking maternity leave?

SUE
Mmm, can't wait!

Barbara nods, encouragingly.

BARBARA
Rest is so important.

SHEBA
Do you know what it is?

Sheba catches Barbara's eye and suggests she put her cigarette out. Barbara does so, but only to please her.

SUE
Rog reckons it's a boy but I'm certain it's a girl. Aren't they supposed to be low slung? I can't believe nobody noticed, I'm fourteen weeks! Didn't you see how chunky I'm getting?!

Barbara notices a dab of froth on Sheba's nose. She hands her a serviette. Sheba thanks her with a smile.

EXT. CHEMIST/STREET – LATER

Barbara and Sheba waiting outside. Sue inside buying a hot-water bottle.

SHEBA
Do you want to come for lunch, on Sunday?

BARBARA
Where?

SHEBA
To mine, to our house.

BARBARA
Won't you be with your family?

SHEBA

Yes, but you're very welcome. It's no big deal, I'll just do a lasagne or something.

BARBARA

I adore lasagne.

Barbara is almost blushing.

INT. DEPARTMENT STORE – SATURDAY

BARBARA
(*voice-over*)

Bliss!

Women's wear. A Shop Assistant nods as Barbara discusses the virtues of a skirt she's interested in.

BARBARA
(*voice-over*)

A merry flag on the Arctic wilderness of my calendar.

Shoe Department. Five different pairs for consideration.

To another Shop Assistant's relief Barbara finally plumps for a pair of black low-heelers with a strap.

INT. HAIRDRESSERS – SAME DAY

Barbara seemingly asleep while the Girl washes her hair.

BARBARA
(*voice-over*)

One must make an effort when one receives an invitation.

She half-opens one eye and sees the Girl making faces. The Girl at the next sink mocks her own customer similarly.

INT. BARBARA'S FLAT – EVENING

Barbara walks into the bedroom in her new heels. She twirls in front of the mirror, 'catching herself'.

BARBARA
(*voice-over*)
The art of it is seeming not to.

Barbara carefully spray starches her white blouse.

INT./EXT. BARBARA'S CAR/STREET — SUNDAY

Barbara cruising down the street looking for a space. Her VW Polo incongruous amongst the smart cars already parked.

BARBARA
(*voice-over*)
Lasagne tends to disagree with my bowels . . .

She parks and takes out her compact, touches up her make-up. She's early. And nervous.

BARBARA
(*voice-over*)
I'll ask for a small portion.

She lights a cigarette. Determined to stay calm.

EXT. SHEBA'S HOUSE — TEN MINUTES LATER

Barbara walks up the front steps of a large Victorian house.

She observes the front garden: a cherry tree, a rusty bike, a mildewed cricket-bat handle impaled in the unkempt grass.

She stands there, pristine in her grey skirt, white blouse, new black heels. She holds a bunch of flowers.

She composes herself and presses the bell. No sound.

She tries again. Waits. Nothing. She tries the knocker.

The door is opened by a tall, slightly shaggy Man in his late fifties.

BARBARA
I think I've come to the wrong house.

MAN
(*smiles*)
No, you're bang on. I'm Richard. Come in!

INT. HALLWAY – CONTINUOUS

BARBARA

I'm so sorry, I thought –

RICHARD

That I'd be twenty years younger and twice as handsome.

He helps her out of her coat.

Sorry, were you out there long? The bell's knackered.

He dumps her coat over the banister. The hall is cluttered with junk, boots, bicycles, etc.

Bash!

A flustered Sheba pokes her head out of the kitchen.

SHEBA

Hi, Barbara! The kitchen's on fire!

Richard raises an eyebrow and ushers Barbara in.

INT. SITTING ROOM – CONTINUOUS

BARBARA

Oh, what a splendid room.

RICHARD

What can I get you? We're semi-pro drinkers here; absinthe, hooch, pick your poison.

BARBARA

Could I have a dry sherry, please?

RICHARD

Erm . . . I might have some apricot brandy knocking around . . .

BARBARA

Or a dry white wine?

RICHARD

Done. Have a seat.

Barbara takes in the room; the look is 'battered bourgeois' – the big sofas, the bare boards, paintings, overflowing bookshelves, Sunday papers.

She sits in an armchair and finds herself semi-recumbent such is its hidden depth. A Girl of fifteen drifts in. She quietly observes as Barbara struggles to sit up.

BARBARA

You must be Polly.

POLLY
(*shrugs*)

Must be. Hi.

BARBARA

I'm Barbara.

POLLY

Hi, Barbara.

Polly's contempt is instantaneous but she makes a vague stab at concealing it.

She flops into a sofa, sips her bottle of Evian.

Are you going somewhere?

BARBARA

Excuse me?

POLLY

You're all poshed up.

BARBARA

Oh . . . I have an appointment. Later. In town. (*Beat.*) Have you always lived here?

POLLY

Mum inherited it. It's her little joke –

RICHARD
(*coming in*)

– I only married her for the property.

He carries an opened bottle of wine and glasses.

RICHARD
(*to Polly*)

Morning.

He hands drinks round.

Did Pete go?

Polly nods.

He was welcome to stay.

POLLY
He's not really into lunch.

RICHARD
(*to Barbara*)

Cheers.

BARBARA
Mmm. What is it?

RICHARD
A witless Chardonnay.

BARBARA
Are you interested in wine?

RICHARD
Only the drinking part. You?

BARBARA
Well, I spent a portion of the summer on the Amalfi coast
and I became –

*She's interrupted by loud thumps as someone thunders down the
wooden stairs.*

RICHARD
Here's trouble . . .

Ben runs in and leaps head first onto the sofa.

Easy, Rocky! Easy!

Ben is twelve. He has Down's Syndrome. Barbara didn't know.

She watches Richard and his son playfully fighting with each other.

> BARBARA
> (*voice-over*)
> I'd anticipated a suave, young lawyer and two perfect
> poppets. Not so. She's married some crumbling patriarch –
> he's nearly as old as me!

INT. KITCHEN – LATER

*Everyone is sitting at the big table, eating their slightly burnt lasagne
and salad.*

*Barbara has a tiny portion, almost untouched. She conceals it with a
large lettuce leaf.*

> BARBARA
> (*voice-over*)
> And then there's the daughter – a pocket princess.

Polly picks at her food, uninterested.

> BARBARA
> (*voice-over*)
> And finally, a somewhat tiresome court jester.

*Ben wolfs his food down, making a mess which Sheba wipes up
habitually.*

> BEN
> I'm going to be a wizard.

> BARBARA
> Oh? . . . Is that when you're a grown-up . . .?

> SHEBA
> No, he's just been cast in his school play!

Ben beams with pride as Sheba hugs him.

> RICHARD
> (*critic's voice*)
> Amongst next year's cultural highlights I greatly look
> forward to Benjamin Hart in the key role of The Wizard.

Indeed, I find myself to be beside myself with anticipation for this doubtless auspicious stage debut.

As Richard continues . . .

> BARBARA
> (*voice-over*)
> A rogue image swam through me, hubby's pruney old mouth pursed at Sheba's breast.

INT. SITTING ROOM – LATER

Sheba and Ben are dancing to 'Funky Kingston' by Toots and the Maytals, up loud on the Bang & Olufsen.

> BARBARA
> (*voice-over*)
> After lunch a rather mortifying family tradition . . .

Sheba's quite drunk and having a ball. Richard moves to his own slower rhythm amusing the delighted Ben.

> BARBARA
> (*voice-over*)
> They do things differently in bourgeois bohemia.

Polly and Barbara, sour bedfellows on the sofa, both mortally embarrassed.

Polly offers Barbara a cigarette, which she accepts gratefully.

As the music continues Barbara's expression changes: her admiration for Sheba's enthusiasm, her love for her son, her natural warmth, her beauty . . .

As Sheba dances Barbara is almost overcome by her.

Richard grooves up and encourages Polly to join in. She bats him away and draws on her Marlboro Light. Now he tries to haul Barbara to her feet; she protests but he's relentless. Polly – the traitor – 'helps' her up.

Barbara stands in the centre of the room. An awkward moment as she half-raises her arms for a formal dance, but Richard's not there to reciprocate.

Ben grabs Barbara's hand and they dance.

A mobile phone rings – unheard by all except Polly. She passes it to her mother.

Sheba goes out into the hallway to speak. Her conversation seems intense, possibly furtive . . .

EXT. GARDEN – LATER

Richard and Ben are playing French Cricket. The garden is large, rambling and overgrown.

Barbara and Sheba head to a partially concealed summerhouse at the back. Sheba carries coffee and biscuits on a tray.

SHEBA
I'm sorry I didn't tell you about Ben – not that it's – Just sometimes people don't quite know how to react.

BARBARA
Not at all, he's charming. (*Beat.*) Has it been difficult?

SHEBA
Well, you just get on with it, don't you? Polly's the tricky one, but who isn't at fifteen? I was impossible.

BARBARA
Surely not!

SHEBA
Wilful and flighty – lethal combination. You?

BARBARA
I think I was rather quiet.

SHEBA
Did you want children?

BARBARA
Mmm. But I never found the time.

They reach the large, bashed-up summerhouse.

BARBARA
How wonderful.

SHEBA

Richard took me away for our wedding anniversary, years
ago. When we got back it was here, as if by magic.

They go inside.

INT. SUMMERHOUSE – CONTINUOUS.

*Barbara sips her coffee, conscious she's in Sheba's 'lair' and feeling
privileged to be so.*

*The 'studio' is full of Sheba's pottery works, drawings and sketches.
A comfy, messy den of curios and artefacts.*

SHEBA

It was supposed to be my studio but it's more of a refuge
really.

BARBARA

A room of one's own.

*There's a big stack of vinyl LPs and seven-inch singles by the stereo.
A large photo pinned to the wall amongst a collage of other images.
Sheba as a teenager with a gang of friends, exotically dressed in post-
punk splendour – heavy eye make-up etc. Threatening, confident, sexy.*

BARBARA

Is this you?

SHEBA

Well . . . it was.

Barbara admires some glazed plates on a shelf.

BARBARA

I like these. Such vibrant colours.

SHEBA

Take one. Take two. Have the lot actually.

BARBARA

Oh, I couldn't possibly.

Sheba takes a few down and hands them to her.

SHEBA

Honestly, no one else wants them.

BARBARA

I'll treasure them.

Too intense, too much – Barbara knows it.

Sheba starts wrapping the plates in old newspaper. Barbara carefully sits on a rickety chair.

BARBARA

It must be exhausting, running a family and teaching as well?

SHEBA

I can't wait for term to end. Roll on Christmas and a month of sod all. Oh, I shouldn't have kidded myself I could teach. I've spent the last ten years looking after Ben – I was desperate to get out and do something – finally we got him into this great local school and I'm free to work and . . .

She shakes her head at the difficulty of it all.

BARBARA

You're going to be a terrific teacher.

SHEBA

Thanks, but I'm bloody hopeless and everyone knows it.

She finishes with the plates and flops into the shabby old sofa.

BARBARA

Children are feral – don't let them sense your anxiety.

SHEBA

How do you cope?

BARBARA

Oh, I'm a battleaxe. I'm not popular but at least they respect me.

SHEBA

Well, you're popular with me.

*Barbara smiles. A hint of therapist and patient. Barbara on her chair,
Sheba on the couch – the hip bone exposed, the ankles, her hands
waving as she continues to talk.*

> BARBARA
> (*voice-over*)
> She spoke of her 'vile' mother, her grief over the death of
> her father, the glory days when Richard scooped her up
> and then jettisoned his wife and children for what she
> called a 'non-stop fuckfest'. It's a peculiar trait of the
> privileged: immediate, incautious intimacy. But Sheba went
> well beyond the tendencies of her class. She was utterly
> candid; a novice confessing to the mother superior.

It's getting dark outside. Richard and Ben have gone in.

*The atmosphere in the summerhouse is intimate now, sisterly. Sheba
concludes her long speech:*

> SHEBA
> But you know, marriage and kids, it's wonderful but it
> doesn't give you meaning. It gives you an imperative but it
> doesn't help you . . . My father used to say – you know, on
> the tube – 'mind the gap' . . .?

Barbara looks a little confused.

> I dunno, the distance between life as you dream it and . . .
> (*Softly.*) . . . life as it is.

Barbara stares at her, rapt.

> BARBARA
> I know exactly what you mean.

INT. SITTING ROOM – THAT NIGHT

Close: a gold star on a page of Barbara's diary.

> BARBARA
> (*voice-over*)
> A gold-star day!

She sticks the star down with her thumb.

BARBARA
(*voice-over*)

I always knew we'd be friends. Out mutual reserve inhibited us, but now it is manifest; a spiritual recognition!

As she continues to write we see the strangely anodyne possessions of her life: the trinkets, the cat toys, etc.

INT. SCHOOL HALL – DAY

Assembly. Pabblem making announcements. The Pupils sit in rows. Staff on a raised platform.

BARBARA
(*voice-over*)

'S' and I share the ability to see through the quotidian awfulness of things. In a different (better) age we would be ladies of leisure: lunching together, visiting galleries, travelling, putting the world to rights.

Barbara sits behind Sheba, who is casually twirling the hair at the back of her neck. A strand falls into Barbara's lap.

BARBARA
(*voice-over*)

We would be companions.

The strand of hair taut between her fingers.

INT. SCHOOL HALL – LATE AFTERNOON (DECEMBER)

The school carol concert. The last day of term.

A school band on stage doing a 'rap' version of 'Hark the Herald Angels Sing'. Toasting each other, the hoods, the attitude.

Sue Hodge is conducting them, gleefully.

Pabblem beams. This is what his school is all about.

Brian is into the groove. He wears a Tottenham Hotspur baseball cap and stuffs a mince pie in his gob.

Gita fakes enjoyment – in common with many other staff.

The Pupils are allowed to 'dress down'. Some are in festive fancy dress. Some clap along. Others throw food around.

Barbara sits at the end of a row. An empty seat beside her. Bill tries to sit in it but Barbara says it's reserved.

She looks around for Sheba. Not here. She slips out of the room.

INT. BARBARA'S CLASSROOM

Barbara goes over to the window and looks out. It's dark outside. There's a dim light on in the Art Studio.

INT. SCHOOL CORRIDOR

Barbara heads for the exit. Christmas decorations and children's art fill the walls.

The rap music echoes down the empty corridor.

EXT. PLAYGROUND

The playground in darkness. Barbara heads towards the Art Studio. The light still on. But then it goes out.

Barbara waits for Sheba to emerge. But she doesn't.

Now Barbara approaches, perplexed . . .

She hears a noise – a chair scraping back – male laughter, a 'shhh' – silence.

Barbara sneaks up to a window. Standing on tiptoe she can just see inside.

Darkness. Footsteps. A murmur . . .

And then . . . a match . . . a tiny flare of light. And then an orange glow – a cigarette.

Still she can't see properly, her eyes beginning to adjust.

She can make out Sheba's desk now . . .

And Sheba sitting on her chair at the desk . . .

Her shirt undone to the waist . . .

Barbara holds her breath.

Sheba's mouth – she's saying something . . .

And now the orange glow comes back into view.

She sees a white shirt. A man holding a cigarette.

Sheba gesturing – something to do with the cigarette . . .

The man stands in front of Sheba.

A playful exchange of words. He puts the cigarette out.

Sheba nods and then undoes his zip. Pulls him towards her.

Barbara watching as Sheba gives head.

The man comes quickly. Sheba's hand on his mouth, silencing him.

Barbara's hand on her own mouth.

Distant applause and stamping. The carol concert's finished.

The lovers hear the applause. They kiss passionately.

Sheba buttons her shirt. He goes to the door and slips out.

Barbara edges round the building to see him . . . It's that boy – fifteen years old – Steven Connolly.

Barbara grips the wall for support.

Steven heads towards the school gates pulling his coat on and lugging his school bag over his shoulder.

The Art Studio lights flash on.

Barbara turns back, sees Sheba picking something from the floor – a cigarette butt. She wraps it in paper and pockets it.

Children and Staff start streaming out of the school doors.

Barbara alone for a moment before she's engulfed.

INT. SITTING ROOM – NIGHT

Barbara sitting in her armchair, still in shock. Thinking.

EXT. SUPERMARKET CAR PARK – DAY

Sheba and Ben loading the car with their shopping. Sheba humps a box of mineral water into the boot.

Her mobile rings; she answers.

> BARBARA
> (*voice-over*)
> It's Barbara. I need to talk to you about Steven Connolly.

Sheba freezes. The best she can do:

> SHEBA
> (*in phone*)
> Who . . .?

Intercut as necessary

INT. SITTING ROOM – SAME TIME

A thin smile from Barbara.

> BARBARA
> (*in phone*)
> Let's not, shall we? I'm afraid I've learnt of your 'activities'.

Sheba – horrified – before she can respond.

> Doubtless you're aware you could go to jail. I'm driving to Eastbourne tonight, I'm spending Christmas with my sister. I'll be with you at five.

Barbara puts the phone down. Silence.

Then, a strange croak. Her cat, Portia, has vomited at her feet.

EXT. SHEBA'S HOUSE – EARLY EVENING

Before Barbara can knock Sheba comes out in her coat.

SHEBA

Let's go to the pub, OK?

BARBARA

I brought you this, for all of you.

Barbara hands her a bottle of sherry. Sheba looks at it like it's a bomb, then deposits it inside the door.

EXT. HIGHGATE STREETS/PUB – MOMENTS LATER

They walk in silence. Sheba sick with fear. Barbara has to double her pace to keep up.

They arrive at the pub. It's festooned with festive cheer. A couple of drunks barge past them singing carols.

Barbara gestures to a wooden table with benches, chained to the wall outside – quieter.

EXT. PUB – LATER

Sheba and Barbara sitting with their drinks – a dry sherry and a hefty scotch. Barbara lights a cigarette. Sheba is shaking with fear (and cold).

SHEBA

So . . . when . . . when will you tell them?

Barbara is inscrutable, relishing her power.

BARBARA

I need to know the circumstances. You must inform me of everything.

Sheba takes a slug of her drink, her only option to comply.

SHEBA

Actually, you were there, when I first noticed him . . .

EXT. PLAYGROUND – FLASHBACK

A roar. Steven scores his goal then whips his shirt off and points in glory at Sheba.

SHEBA
(*voice-over*)
I think you gave him a telling off.

BARBARA
(*voice-over*)
No, I gave him a slight ticking off.

Sheba gives Steven a little smile.

SHEBA
(*voice-over*)
He dedicated his goal to me. It was just a sweet thing,
it amused me.

Steven runs off past Barbara who tells him to put his shirt back on.

But Sheba continues to gaze at the boy – his smooth skin, his hips, his muscles moving as he pulls the shirt over his head.

INT. ART STUDIO – AFTERNOON

Sheba alone, repairing her torn posters.

SHEBA
(*voice-over*)
A few days later he came to see me.

Steven comes in carrying a large envelope.

STEVEN
Miss, would you look at my drawings, please?

SHEBA
I'll look at them in class. You do Art, don't you?

STEVEN
I'm not allowed . . . (*Embarrassed.*) I'm special needs. I gotta
do extra reading instead.

SHEBA
You did these at home?

He nods and hands her the envelope.

Sheba looks at the boy's 'work'. Pencil sketches of fruit, a can of Coke, a woman vaguely like herself, his own hands . . .

These are good. You can draw.

Steven is thrilled.

Hands are very difficult, aren't they?

> STEVEN
> Yeah, they're a right bastard.

> SHEBA
> You have to really study them, the bone structure . . . look . . .

She does a quick sketch of his hands. She's talented, deft. Her sketch is simple but clear.

> STEVEN
> Can I keep it, Miss?

She hands it to him – unsure if she's already crossed a line.

> SHEBA
> (*voice-over*)
> I told him I'd speak to the Deputy Head, look into his timetable.

INT. CORRIDOR – DAY

Sheba with Ted Mawson. Kids streaming past between lessons.

> TED
> If we started pulling strings for one child the whole system would unravel.

> SHEBA
> But he's talented, he's actually found something he believes in!

> TED
> Oh, they're all talented.

Cut back to:

EXT. PUB – EVENING

Sheba and Barbara at their table. Barbara looks steely.

                    BARBARA
You'd found your 'gem', as Sue would say?

                    SHEBA
I said I'd teach him after school, but only if he felt like it.
It's our job, isn't it?

                    BARBARA
Within specified hours and a specified curriculum.

                    SHEBA
He came every day for two weeks. Yes, I was flattered, but
more than that, I was excited to find someone who actually
wanted to learn.

                    BARBARA
But you must've suspected his motives?

INT. ART STUDIO – DAY

Sheba showing Steven a book of Da Vinci's drawings.

                    SHEBA
                   (*voice-over*)
I sensed he had a little crush on me, but so what? It was
innocent.

                    STEVEN
So he invented a sort of helicopter five hundred years ago?
Does your brain in.

Sheba smiles, charmed by him.

Another day: Steven's new drawing of his hands. A slight improvement.

                    SHEBA
That's so much better. Look, you've absolutely got that
knuckle.

                    STEVEN
                   (*grins*)
Nailed it.

36

She's pleased for him and ruffles his hair. Mistake. She knows it instantly.

                        STEVEN
Do that again, Miss.

                        SHEBA
Don't be silly. Off you go.

She gets up, starts tidying, pushing chairs under desks. He leaps up to help her.

                        STEVEN
What you having for tea, Miss?

                        SHEBA
I don't know, I'll probably buy something on the way home.

                        STEVEN
Are you a good cook?

                        SHEBA
Not really.

                        STEVEN
You suck?

Pause. She narrows her eyes.

                        SHEBA
Go home, Steven.

He stares at her and then leaves. Sheba puts on her coat.

                        BARBARA
                        (*voice-over*)
That's when you should've stopped it.

INT. OUTSIDE SPORTS HALL – DAY

                        SHEBA
                        (*voice-over*)
I did! I told him I wouldn't teach him any more.

Busy lobby area. Sheba comes out of a meeting, carrying papers and files.

Steven, in sports kit, suddenly throws her a football.

> STEVEN

Miss!

Sheba catches it and sternly hands it back to him.

> SHEBA
> (*voice-over*)

He wouldn't accept it. He just kept coming back.

EXT. STREET – ANOTHER DAY

Sheba cycling home. She passes Steven in the street. He gazes at her.

> SHEBA
> (*voice-over*)

It began to feel like 'our secret'. And secrets can be seductive . . .

EXT. DELICATESSEN/STREET – ANOTHER DAY

Sheba comes out with a bag of shopping. Steven is polishing her saddle with his sleeve. He finishes with a flourish and stands back gesturing for her to alight.

She dumps her bag in the bike basket.

> SHEBA

What are you doing here?

> STEVEN

I live here.

He gestures to the tower blocks of a grim-looking estate.

'S all right, apart from the crack'eads and that. Some bloke got stabbed last week.

Sheba looks concerned. He steadies the bike as she fiddles with the chunky lock.

SHEBA

I'm going now. Good day to you, young man.

STEVEN

D'you wanna come for a walk?

SHEBA

Absolutely not! I'm going home to my family. As should you.

She climbs on the bike. He's still holding the handlebars.

STEVEN

My dad's got the hump. He got sacked, been taking it out on me.

He gestures with his arm, Sheba looks shocked.

SHEBA

He hits you?

Steven vaguely nods, embarrassed.

Does your mother know?

STEVEN
(*shakes head*)
She's got this kidney problem, been waiting months for an operation. I don't wanna give her more grief.

SHEBA

You could call the Social Services. They'll come and see him, give him a warning.

STEVEN
(*shrugs*)
I'll be all right.

SHEBA

If he does it again you tell me, OK?

STEVEN

Thanks, Miss.

She looks at him, full of sympathy. He leans in and holds her face.

You're beautiful, Miss. You don't know how beautiful you are.

Before she can respond he's on his way.

EXT. PUB — EVENING

Barbara looks at Sheba reproachfully.

                    SHEBA
              (*desperately explaining*)
My heart went out to him . . . he was so vulnerable. I knew
it was wrong and immoral and completely ridiculous but . . .
I don't know . . . I just . . . allowed it to happen.

                    BARBARA
The boy is fifteen!

                    SHEBA
But he's quite mature for his age.

                    BARBARA
'But' is not a helpful word here! He's a minor and you've
broken the law.

Sheba nods, chastened. Pupil to teacher.

                    SHEBA
This'll sound sick, but something in me felt . . . entitled.

INT. SCHOOL CORRIDOR — DAY

Between lessons. Staff and Pupils coming in and out of classrooms.

                    SHEBA
                 (*voice-over*)
I've been good all my adult life: decent wife, dutiful
mother, coping with Ben . . .

*Steven passes Sheba in the crush of bodies; he slips her a handwritten
note.*

INT. ART STUDIO — LATER

*Sheba struggling to control her class as they splatter each other with
paint.*

SHEBA
(*voice-over*)

This voice inside me was going, 'Why shouldn't you be
bad?'

She sits at her desk and reads the note: MEET ME AT 8 TONIGHT.
PLEASE. *His mobile number is scrawled below it.*

INT. SHEBA'S HOUSE, SITTING ROOM/HALL – THAT EVENING.

Sheba in an armchair with a glass of wine.

SHEBA
(*voice-over*)

'Why shouldn't you transgress? You've earned the right.'

Ben is watching TV with Richard. Sheba checks her watch: 7.45.

*She stares at her husband and son. She decides. She gets up, ruffles
Ben's hair, kisses him on the top of the head.*

SHEBA

Sue phoned, OK if I go for a drink?

RICHARD

Sure. I'll put bugalugs to bed.

He tickles Ben as Sheba goes out into the hall.

She checks herself in the mirror.

*Polly emerges from the kitchen, talking intensely on her mobile. Sheba
flinches, somehow feeling 'caught'.*

SHEBA

I'm just going for a drink, with Sue.

Polly points to her phone 'I'm busy' – and slopes upstairs.

EXT. PUB

BARBARA

Why Sue?

Sheba gulps her scotch, feeling the cold.

SHEBA

Dunno, first person I thought of.

On Barbara: disappointed.

EXT. RAILWAY ARCH – NIGHT

Sheba locks her bike to a railing. She makes her way to the meeting place, giddy with anticipation.

SHEBA
(*voice-over*)

I remembered that gorgeous feeling, like being sixteen. I'm going to give you what you want and you don't know it yet.

Steven is waiting there, smoking.

STEVEN

Evening, Miss.

She looks him in the eye.

SHEBA

Have you done this before?

He nods but his cockiness is slightly diminished.

STEVEN

Not with someone like you, I mean . . . a proper woman.

She touches his cheek, tenderly. They walk together.

EXT. DISUSED RAILWAY YARD – NIGHT

Sheba follows Steven down an 'alley' between a disused train and a siding.

Steven stops. A clearing. He puts his coat down.

STEVEN

Make yourself comfortable.

He looks at Sheba, barely believing his luck.

SHEBA

It's incredibly important that we keep this secret. Does anyone know you're here?

STEVEN

No.

SHEBA

You can't tell anyone, ever.

She stares at him. He takes her hand, soothes her . . .

STEVEN

Miss, I'm no genius but I ain't no dickhead. I won't tell anyone. You can trust me.

SHEBA
(*distantly*)

We'd both get into terrible trouble.

Steven looks into her eyes. She kisses him. They fall onto the ground. They start making out like teenagers – laughter, gasps and elbow banging.

SHEBA
(*voice-over*)

It was easy. Like having another drink when you know you shouldn't.

Sheba and Steven fucking. Semi-clothed. It's very quick.

STEVEN

Miss?

SHEBA

What?

He murmurs in her ear.

What? (*He murmurs again.*) What?!

STEVEN

Can I come inside you?

SHEBA

Yes!

And he does. Sheba holds him tight.

Later: Steven lies on her stomach. She strokes his hair. He reaches for his cigarettes. Thinks.

STEVEN
Can I smoke, Miss?

SHEBA
You can do what you want. But enough of this 'Miss'.

He grins. Lights a cigarette, offers her one, she shakes her head. Steven cracks open a can of beer and offers her the other. She takes it and swigs some. He watches her intently.

STEVEN
Were you a model once?

Sheba shakes her head.

You shoulda been. You're well fit.

SHEBA
'Gosh but don't I know it.'

STEVEN
You're into The Streets?!

SHEBA
My daughter is.

STEVEN
She the same age as me?

SHEBA
None of your beeswax.

He's smart enough not to persist.

STEVEN
Anyway, the point is you're fit.

SHEBA
Well, so are you.

STEVEN
You reckon? My sister says I look like a bollock with measles.

44

SHEBA
(*shakes her head*)
You've done my brain in.

They toast each other in the moonlight.

It's freezing cold and they start to button up their clothes. But Steven can't bear to let her go; he stops her doing up her shirt, kisses her.

STEVEN
You wanna do it again?

Sheba smiles. Men can't do this.

What? What?

She laughs, then sees he's getting upset.

SHEBA
Yes. I want to do it again.

She pulls him towards her and feels his cock.

I want to do it again.

INT. SHEBA'S HOUSE – THAT NIGHT

Sheba parks her bike in the hall. As she checks herself in the mirror, an angry voice from the sitting room:

RICHARD
(*out of shot*)
Oh, you TART! You feckless bitch!

Sheba freezes – then realises he's shouting at the TV.

She goes into the sitting room. Richard is slobbed out on the sofa, remote control perched on his belly. He raises an arm in greeting.

RICHARD
I'm dying! These people are killing me! I'm having a coronary right here on this sofa.

SHEBA
Coffee?

RICHARD

Love one. Add a vat of scotch will you? (*At TV.*) ANSWER
THE QUESTION! It's 'yes' or 'no', you dozy old bastard!

SHEBA
(*amused*)

Change channels.

She goes into the kitchen.

RICHARD

I keep flipping back. I'm in an orgy of masochism.

Sheba starts making coffee.

*The fridge with its collage of family photos and school schedules. The
clutter of family life . . .*

EXT. PUB — NIGHT

Barbara stubs another cigarette out, she's realised something.

BARBARA

The day we met, it had already begun?

INT. SCHOOL CORRIDOR — FLASHBACK

*The 'Homework Club' day. Steven and Davis getting a dressing down
from Barbara as Sheba watches.*

SHEBA
(*voice-over*)

Yes.

BARBARA
(*voice-over*)

You had further relations that day?

EXT. PUB — NIGHT

Sheba thinks: truth is best policy here.

SHEBA

We went to the Art Room.

BARBARA

Well, I'm glad I was such an aphrodisiac. I was trying to
help you.

SHEBA

And you did. I'm incredibly grateful. You've been such a
good friend.

BARBARA
(*quietly*)
Not reciprocated, it seems.

*Sheba suddenly sees that Barbara's anger is personal – and potentially
explosive. She proceeds carefully . . .*

SHEBA

I desperately wanted to confess to you. But how could I? . . .
Barbara . . . ?

She waits until Barbara looks at her.

It would've put you in an impossible situation. But I so
wish I had. You'd have made me see sense.

Barbara considers: is Sheba 'playing' her? No, impossible.

They sit in silence. Barbara watches Sheba – then blinks:

BARBARA
(*voice-over*)
And then I realised my fury had blinded me . . .

SHEBA

Do we need more drinks?

Barbara nods, miles away.

But can we go inside? I'm freezing.

BARBARA
(*voice-over*)
There was a magnificent opportunity here . . .

INT. PUB – MOMENTS LATER

Sheba at the bar, Barbara at a table.

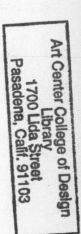

47

BARBARA
(*voice-over*)

With stealth I might secure the prize, long term, forever in my debt . . .

Sheba heads back to Barbara carrying the new drinks.

BARBARA
(*voice-over*)

I could gain everything. By doing . . . nothing.

Sheba sits, fraught with anxiety. Barbara lights a cigarette.

SHEBA

I . . . I know you have to tell them; the Head, the school, whoever. All I ask is you wait till the New Year? I'm begging you, please, let me have this Christmas with my family . . . ?

She's almost in tears. Barbara stares at her. Then smiles.

BARBARA

I think you've misunderstood me. (*Beat.*) I'm your friend. We're friends.

SHEBA

I know. Of course. But . . .

BARBARA

Oh, you poor thing, have you got yourself in a terrible state? I'm not going to report you. I only want to help you, to support you through this.

She gives Sheba a tender squeeze on the hand.

SHEBA

You're not going to tell?

Barbara shakes her head. Sheba is overcome with relief.

You won't tell anyone?

BARBARA

Who would it benefit? Not you nor the boy and certainly not the school. No. It's a private matter and we must keep it so.

SHEBA

Yes – maybe I should resign?

BARBARA

No, no, no! That might alert suspicion. You must stay at the school, but the affair has to end.

Sheba nods.

Immediately. Your solemn promise. I can't help you unless you promise.

Sheba realises that Barbara means it literally.

SHEBA

I – I promise.

BARBARA

Will it be difficult?

Sheba stares into her glass.

SHEBA

He'll be very upset. He comes from such a . . . loveless home.

BARBARA

You're not in love?

Sheba looks up, an innocent. She gives a slight nod. Barbara tries not to react but is clearly shocked.

SHEBA

I know it's appalling and illegal and unethical but I'm hopelessly besotted.

Barbara looks vaguely sick.

Sorry. When you're in love you want to tell the whole world about it.

BARBARA

I wouldn't, though.

They manage to share a grim smile.

But isn't it . . . just a physical thing, mainly?

49

SHEBA

Well . . . (*Raises an eyebrow.*) I can't tell you.

BARBARA

I think you just have.

SHEBA

Do you know what I'm talking about?

BARBARA

Well, I've read quite a bit of D. H. Lawrence.

EXT. PUB/STREET − LATER

Barbara and Sheba walking.

BARBARA
(*voice-over*)
I played the maiden aunt but I'm well aware of the
proclivities of the fifteen-year-old male. Even I have been
the subject of their graffitied yearnings in the school toilets.
By law they are children, but their grim, pungent urges are
entirely adult.

They arrive at Barbara's car.

BARBARA

So you'll tell him straight after Christmas?

Sheba nods, determinedly.

All for the best.

SHEBA

I know. Thank you so much. You've been so brilliant.

BARBARA

And you'll tell me when it's done?

SHEBA

Yes.

*A big hug. Then Sheba sees the travelling cat box on the passenger
seat. Portia is asleep.*

You never said . . .

BARBARA

Standard issue for spinsters. (*Frowns.*) She's been off her food recently, I'm a bit worried about her . . .

SHEBA

There's a terrific vet up the road, he was great with Ben's rabbit.

Barbara lingers, relishing this time with Sheba.

BARBARA

Have you got many people coming tomorrow?

SHEBA

Mmm, my lot, Richard's lot – including first wife.

They share a grimace.

BARBARA

And your mother?

SHEBA

Oh yes.

A second grimace.

BARBARA

Well, happy Christmas.

SHEBA

You too. And thank you.

BARBARA

Courage, mon brave!

Barbara gets in her car.

BARBARA
(*voice-over*)

And *bon voyage* to her little leprechaun.

Barbara drives off as Sheba heads back to her house.

BARBARA
(*voice-over*)

Sheba and I share a deep understanding now.

INT. SHEBA'S HOUSE – CONTINUOUS

Sheba composes herself in the hall and then goes into the sitting room.

> BARBARA
> (*voice-over*)
> No one can violate our magnificent complicity.

Richard is wrapping a present. He turns with the ineptly wrapped package, taunts her with it.

> RICHARD
> Ha!

She tries to steal it from him.

> Don't snatch! Wait till tomorrow!

He chucks the present under the Christmas tree.

> You've been gone ages.

> SHEBA
> Oh, Barbara was . . . just some school thing.

He pours some wine for them.

> How's his nibs?

> RICHARD
> Still awake, madly excited, I said he could wait up for you.

> SHEBA
> And her ladyship?

> RICHARD
> (*points upstairs*)
> 'Depressed'. Pete phoned. They had a barney, he's not coming tomorrow.

They share a moment of parental sadness.

> SHEBA
> Do you think he's bad news?

> RICHARD
> Well, these older men can be very dodgy.

She smiles, suddenly kisses him, passionately. Richard is slightly surprised but responds in kind.

INT. POLLY'S BEDROOM – LATER

Polly is lying on her bed, iPod on, smoking. She's been crying. Sheba sits with her.

> POLLY
>
> Did Daddy tell you?

Sheba nods.

> He's gonna bin me, I know it.

> SHEBA
>
> You're very lovely and he's clever enough to appreciate it.

> POLLY
>
> I'm fat as fuck, Mum.

> SHEBA
>
> He'll be back.

> POLLY
>
> I can't live without him.

Sheba holds her. The girl resists a little but then succumbs – grateful for the contact.

EXT. GRAND HOTEL, EASTBOURNE – CHRISTMAS DAY

Establishing shot.

The sea. The promenade. The white stuccoed Regency hotel.

Sounds of festive music from a jazz combo.

INT. DINING ROOM – SAME TIME

A huge ornate room packed with the elderly, the infirm and their families. A small band playing on a raised area.

Barbara surveys the room: an old man spilling his soup, an old woman tottering in on her crutches, an elderly couple struggling to pull their cracker.

She's mid-lunch with her family: her sister Marjorie, with husband Dave, also their daughter Lorraine and her husband Martin. They all wear paper hats.

Barbara is deep in thought, ruminating on Sheba . . .

> BARBARA
> (*voice-over*)
> Her fetish for the boy was simply her snobbery manifested: 'He's working class and he likes Art.' As if he were a monkey who'd just strolled out of the rain forest and asked for a gin and tonic.

She straightens her paper crown, oblivious to everything.

> DAVE
> Ba! Wakey-wakey!

> MARJORIE
> Lorraine was asking if you'd heard from that nice friend of yours?

> BARBARA
> (*confused*)
> Who?

> LORRAINE
> Jennifer.

> BARBARA
> Oh . . . yes. She left the school, she's teaching at a primary in Stoke. There's a chap apparently. I heard they're engaged.

Lorraine and Martin stifle a giggle but Barbara's seen it. She bides her time . . .

> BARBARA
> How's your eczema, Martin?

He shakes his head, a sad look in his eyes.

> MARTIN
> Bit grim. But Lorraine's found this top specialist in Hastings.

LORRAINE

He's state of the art. He'll give it a really good bash in the
New Year.

*She puts an arm round her disconsolate husband. Barbara eyeballs the
hapless couple.*

BARBARA

It must be so distressing – for both of you.

Marjorie squeezes her son-in-law's crusty hand.

MARJORIE

You've been in my prayers all year.

BARBARA

Fingers crossed for a Christmas miracle.

DAVE
(*raises his glass*)
And so say all of us!

INT. KITCHEN, SHEBA'S HOUSE – SAME TIME

In contrast: noise, hubbub and mayhem. Booze, food, mess.

*Round the big table: Richard, Polly, Ben. Richard's first wife Marcia
and their daughters Saskia and Claire. Sheba's older brother Eddie
with his wife and their infant boys.*

*Sitting next to Ben, Sheba's mother (Mrs Taylor) – a formidable
woman in her sixties.*

*Sheba gets up, gives Polly a little squeeze, then fetches more cream
from the fridge.*

Her mobile beeps, a text message. She reads: HAPPY XMAS MISS!
WISH I WOZ FUCKING U BLIND RITE NOW.

*Sheba looks around – her mother is watching her. She deletes the
message and turns off the phone.*

INT. SHEBA'S HOUSE – EVENING

Sheba outside the half-open sitting-room door with a tray of coffees. Sheba's mother is sitting with Marcia.

> MRS TAYLOR
> Her father was an exceptional man. Exceptional. Bathsheba's a loner I'm afraid. She's beautiful (thank God) – and it's got her through – but it's not quite the same as possessing substance.

Sheba listening in horror.

> MARCIA
> Mmm, strong personality, weak character.

> MRS TAYLOR
> She's a time bomb, actually. Non-bonders are always dangerous.

Marcia nods, knowingly. Sheba is really stung. But she goes in with the tray.

The women smile as she serves them their coffee.

EXT. SHEBA'S HOUSE – EVENING

Sheba comes out of the front door and down the steps with two black bin-liners crammed full of rubbish.

As she's stuffing the bags into the front bins:

> STEVEN
> Happy Christmas.

Steven is lurking near the car. He hands her a little package. Sheba glances at the house – the front door is open.

> SHEBA
> Everyone's inside! Please, you have to go!

> STEVEN
> Aren't you gonna open it?

She quickly opens the package.

> It's made of real fake gold.

It's a cheap, gold necklace with an 'S' on it. It glints in her hand. She's touched by the gesture.

SHEBA

Thank you.

STEVEN

What's up? I haven't heard from you . . .

She motions him back to the side of the house where it's hidden from the front door.

SHEBA

I – I can't see you any more – I'm sorry – I'm really sorry.

She's beside herself. He pulls her towards him.

I can't, it's over.

STEVEN

Why?

RICHARD
(*out of shot*)

Bash?!

They freeze. Richard's legs appear above them at the top of the outside stairs. Then a bag of rubbish.

RICHARD

Bash? (*To someone inside.*) She's not here!

Richard dumps the bag on the doorstep, groaning a bit with drunk exhaustion.

Oh, sod it.

He goes inside, closing the front door behind him.

STEVEN
(*innocently*)

Was that your dad?

Sheba is stunned.

SHEBA

No. He . . . he's my uncle . . .

She stares at Steven. Lost. He returns her gaze.

STEVEN

D'you wanna end it?

SHEBA

I – I – Don't look at me like that.

STEVEN

Have you gone off me?

SHEBA

No – I – You should go. Please. Don't . . . just . . . you have to go now.

He strokes her cheek, she catches his hand.

It's stupid.

He gives her a slight grin.

Go away.

He shakes his head.

Go.

She struggles with herself. He kisses her and she suddenly responds. She clutches the necklace.

INT. HOUSE – MINUTES LATER

Sheba comes in and nearly bumps into Polly, who's heading upstairs – she's on her mobile.

SHEBA

Is it him?

Polly nods happily and climbs the stairs, still talking. Sheba watches her daughter go – natural teenage love.

Sheba goes into the kitchen, contemplates the necklace. One of Eddie's kids runs in. Sheba stuffs the necklace into her pocket. The boy runs out with the plastic cup he was looking for.

Sheba loads dirty crockery into the dishwasher.

Family noises from the sitting room.

She takes out a sachet of detergent, opens it with her teeth. She stares at the hard tablet, the little ball in its centre.

She breaks down, kneeling at the machine, retching with sobs.

> BARBARA
> (*voice-over*)
> I long to phone 'S' but it's late.

INT. SPARE ROOM, MARJORIE'S HOUSE – NIGHT

Barbara at a little dressing table, writing her journal.

> BARBARA
> (*voice-over*)
> Poor girl, all alone with her awful family.

Above her a framed silkscreen print of 'The Last Supper'. Portia lies on the bed, whimpering a little.

> BARBARA
> (*voice-over*)
> Our lives are acutely similar in so many respects.

A knock at the door. Barbara annoyed at the interruption.

> MARJORIE
> (*out of shot*)
> Sis?

Marjorie comes in, wearing her nightie. Sees Portia, coos at her and then strokes the cat as an excuse to enter.

> MARJORIE
> Writing the old diary? I can't imagine how you keep at it.
> I'd have nothing to say.

Marjorie sits on the bed, settling in for a sisterly chat.

> You know you're welcome whenever you want? Not just
> once a year.

> BARBARA
> It's just . . . I'm rather busy at the moment.

MARJORIE

Your racy London life. I'm glad it's so full. (*Pause.*) I'm
sorry about Jennifer. She was lovely.

Barbara flinches a touch.

Is there anyone else . . . someone else who's special?

Silence.

BARBARA

I don't know what you mean.

MARJORIE

I didn't mean to pry.

Barbara stares her out.

Well, goodnight.

BARBARA

To you too.

Marjorie goes. Barbara reflects, a stab of regret.

EXT. RAILWAY YARD – NIGHT

Sheba and Steven, half-dressed, fucking like horny rabbits.

*They lie in each other's arms. Steven toys with the 'S' necklace, happy
she's wearing it.*

INT. PIZZA EXPRESS – DAY

*Barbara and Sheba with menus. Barbara glances over hers, catches
Sheba's eye.*

BARBARA

Are we ladies who lunch?

SHEBA

I think we must be.

Barbara twinkles with delight.

Oh, belated Christmas present.

She takes a beautifully wrapped package out of her bag.

BARBARA

Thank you! Shall I open it?

SHEBA

Silly not to.

Barbara unwraps it, savouring the ribbons, cooing over the smart wrapping paper.

BARBARA

Oh my word, Asprey.

She takes out a sterling silver photo frame engraved with the name 'Portia'.

Barbara can barely speak, just nods in gratitude.

SHEBA

How is she?

Barbara shakes her head, Sheba gives her a consoling squeeze.

BARBARA

You're the most wonderful friend.

INT. SUMMERHOUSE – NIGHT

Sheba and Steven lying, post-coital, on the sofa.

SHEBA

Don't fall asleep.

He opens his eyes, looks around.

STEVEN

Bit close to home, isn't it?

SHEBA

Well, Little Lord Fauntleroy complained of brambles up his arse.

He grins, thinks, animal instinct at work.

STEVEN

Yeah . . . but d'you wanna get caught?

SHEBA

No!

STEVEN

Course you do. Trash it all.

SHEBA

Why would I want to do that?

He's not sure he wants to explore this, jokes instead:

STEVEN

So you can be with me.

She digs him in the ribs.

SHEBA

You're cocky.

STEVEN

You love it.

He gently disengages from her arms, gets up, looks around, exploring her territory.

He turns back: she's deep in thought, considering what he's suggested.

I was only making conversation. It's polite to talk after sex, so's I don't feel like a slut.

He wanders over to her record collection. Sheba pulls on her sweater and comes over to him. He's looking at 'Kaleidoscope' by Siouxsie and the Banshees.

Any good?

SHEBA

It's a masterpiece. Don't they teach you anything?

Sheba strokes his naked back, stares at the record cover.

We used to worship her . . . we were children . . . she made us feel invincible . . .

She's sixteen again. Lost in the memory of it.

Steven wanders over to her work table. There's a half-completed wizard's hat on it. He tries it on. A comical figure in his pants, socks and pointed hat.

> SHEBA
> (*smiling*)
>
> Take it off.

> STEVEN
>
> What's it for?

> SHEBA
>
> Take it off, please. I'm still making it.

> STEVEN
>
> Yeah, but why?

> SHEBA
>
> It's for my son.

> STEVEN
>
> But he's twelve, isn't he?

> SHEBA
>
> He's got Down's Syndrome.

Pause.

> STEVEN
>
> You never said. Sorry.

He takes the hat off, puts it back on the table.

Sheba turns away, not wanting to burden him with her sadness.

He looks at her, suddenly knows he's way out of his depth.

INT. KITCHEN – SATURDAY MORNING

Barbara saunters in carrying her shopping. She stops short, horrified.

Portia is lying on the floor in a pool of urine and vomit.

INT. VET'S SURGERY – LATER

The Vet has just told Barbara the news.

VET

I'm sure she's had a very happy life.

BARBARA

Oh, yes. She has. Thank you.

She strokes Portia as the Vet continues to talk.

INT. SHEBA'S KITCHEN – LATER

Barbara sitting at the table, tears in her eyes. Sheba plies her with scotch.

SHEBA

You've had a terrible shock.

Barbara drinks some more.

BARBARA

Where's Richard? I don't want to disturb your weekend.

SHEBA

It's fine, everyone's out.

Sheba's mobile rings. They both stare at it. Sheba presses BUSY – *looks a touch anxious.*

Can they treat her?

BARBARA

He says it's a matter of weeks . . .

She's recovering now, embarrassed by her tears.

Oh, she's only a pet.

SHEBA

I cried for weeks when our dog died. Weeks!

BARBARA

One does get so attached.

Barbara dries her eyes with a tissue.

I should leave you in peace . . .

Not what Barbara wants but Sheba stands to facilitate it.

SHEBA

Yuh, well . . .

She's in a tight T-shirt, arms bare. Her 'S' necklace on.

Barbara gazes – takes in Sheba's make-up: red lips, dark eye-liner – an echo of her youth.

BARBARA

I like that top. It suits you.

SHEBA

Oh, thanks.

Sheba edges to the door, hinting. But Barbara lingers. She speaks very softly . . . gently . . .

BARBARA

When I was at school, if one of us had had some bad news or was feeling a bit down . . . we used to stroke each other. One of us would do one arm and someone else the other . . . it's the most wonderful sensation. Did you do that at your school?

Sheba shakes her head.

It's incredibly relaxing. For the giver and the receiver . . .

Barbara approaches. Sheba's arms are crossed. Barbara gently uncrosses them, holds her hands.

Close your eyes.

Sheba frowns.

Please. It doesn't work if you don't.

Sheba closes her eyes, knowing this is 'the deal'.

Barbara holds Sheba's hands in hers and then stretches out her arms, palms upwards.

Good.

Barbara begins to run her fingertips gently along Sheba's bare forearms. Up and down.

Sheba is in a silent rictus of embarrassment.

Barbara continues. All the while gazing at Sheba's face, her breasts beneath the tight T-shirt, her arms . . .

There's a good girl.

Sheba opens her eyes, tries to remain polite . . .

SHEBA

I think that's enough.

BARBARA

Close your eyes.

SHEBA
(*firmly*)
I really think that's enough, Barbara.

She stares her out. Barbara stands her ground but is wretched with humiliation.

But now her focus changes from Sheba's face to over her shoulder.

BARBARA

There's someone in your garden!

She points through the French windows. Sheba turns. At the foot of the garden a figure jumps down from the back wall and slips into the summerhouse.

A thief – he came over the wall!

SHEBA

Oh – it'll be one of the neighbours' boys, lost his ball.

Sheba knows it's Steven – prays he stays put.

BARBARA

No, he's gone into your summerhouse – quick, phone the police!

SHEBA

It's just a kid from next door, forget it!

Sheba's mobile rings again. They both stare at it – Sheba paralysed. And now Barbara twigs it. She snatches the phone and answers:

STEVEN
(*voice-over*)
Where are you? I want your hot, sweet cunt right now!

Barbara listens, sickness rising in her. She hands the phone to Sheba.

SHEBA
(*in phone*)
Richard just called, he's on his way – I can't – I'll call you.

As she speaks Barbara collects her bag and storms to the front door, Sheba sprints after her.

Barbara!

EXT. STREET – CONTINUOUS

Barbara's heading for her car. Sheba catches up.

SHEBA
I'm sorry, Ba. I tried to end it, honestly, I – I just couldn't!

Barbara fumbles for her car keys, fighting back tears.

BARBARA
I risked everything for you and in return you humiliate me.

SHEBA
I – I – didn't mean to upset you. Please – I need your help more than ever now – please, don't go!

Barbara opens the car door.

BARBARA
You promised you'd end it – why didn't you?

SHEBA
Because . . .

BARBARA
(*witheringly*)
You're 'in love'?

SHEBA
I – I –

And the child? Do you imagine he reciprocates your soppy 'feelings'? Oh I dare say he's fascinated by the neurotic compulsions of a middle-class lady with marital problems!

SHEBA

Ba –

BARBARA

There's nothing crueller than the adolescent boy, I know them! Once he's had his fill he'll discard you like an old rag –

SHEBA

Ba –

BARBARA

– and revert to rutting with schoolgirls. YOU ARE NOT YOUNG! (*Beat.*) I say this to help you.

Sheba is too stunned to respond.

End it now.

SHEBA

Erm . . . yes – I – I'm thinking . . .

BARBARA

Don't think – DO! DO! DO! DO! (*Beat.*) Or shall I sit here polishing my nails until your husband returns?

SHEBA

No – no – please – I'll do it, I promise.

BARBARA

So what are you waiting for?

Barbara gets in her car and drives off.

EXT. STREET – TEN MINUTES LATER

Sheba on her bike, speeding towards Steven's home.

EXT. COUNCIL ESTATE

Sheba gets off her bike, starts pushing it.

To her surprise it's a clean street, well-kept blocks and houses. Not the sink estate she'd imagined – or been told of.

Kids riding around on bikes. She asks them if they know Steven Connolly. They point her in the right direction.

She finds his home – not the tower block but an ordinary maisonette. She rings the bell.

Mr Connolly opens the door. He's a slight man without an ounce of aggression in him. She'd expected tattoos and brutality.

> SHEBA
> Mr Connolly? I'm Mrs Hart, from St George's – Steven's not in trouble. I just need to see him about . . . an Art project and I was in the area so . . .

> MR CONNOLLY
> (*amiably*)
> Of course, come in, come in!

He shows her in.

> Very good of you to give him these extra lessons. (*Calls upstairs.*) Steve! Visitor!

He's holding a remote control. He gestures into the sitting room where there's a massive TV set, the screen image paused.

> I'm watching *Amelie*. (*Nods, moved.*) Have you seen it?

Sheba shakes her head.

> (*Calls up.*) Steve! Mrs Hart's here! (*To Sheba.*) Probably on his mobile, usually is. Why don't you go up? First door on the right, probably best to knock.

He goes back into the front room.

Sheba climbs the stairs. The house is spotless. Framed school photos line the walls and there are family shots of Steven with his parents and two sisters.

She finds his bedroom door. It says STEVE'S GAFF *in letters cut out from different magazines, punk style.*

She hears his voice, knocks and goes in. He's astonished.

> STEVEN
> (*in phone*)
> Call you back, OK? Laters.

They look at each other.

Sheba takes in the adolescent room, shocked at its 'childishness': the music posters, football paraphernalia, the kid's duvet and strewn clothes.

EXT. COUNCIL ESTATE – MINUTES LATER

Sheba pushing her bike. Steven smoking, edgy.

> SHEBA
> So that's your vicious father?

> STEVEN
> (*shrugs*)
> You wanted a sob story, I gave it you. Made you feel like Bob Geldof.

> SHEBA
> You lied to me!

> STEVEN
> Oooh, sorry, Miss. D'you prefer it if I lived in a shit'ole?

> SHEBA
> And your mother?

> STEVEN
> (*sniffs*)
> I think she's gonna pull through. What d'you want, what you doing here?

And now she has to tell him.

EXT. PLAY AREA/COUNCIL ESTATE – LATER

Steven sits on a swing, flicking at his cigarette in fury.

STEVEN

They're gonna expel me now!

SHEBA

No they won't. I'll get the blame if she tells.

STEVEN

As if she won't?

SHEBA

She likes me, she might not.

STEVEN

Likes you how? Like 'that'? You giving her one 'n' all?

SHEBA
(*snaps*)
Why are you being so cruel? Why, Steven?

He's chastened. He swings slowly to and away from her.

STEVEN

I really like you. You're a nice person and you've been cool.
And it's been great, OK? But it was s'posed to be fun. Now
it's like this serious thing. Whatever shit you're working
out, you know; your husband, your kid, you – I dunno . . .
I can't help you.

Sheba manages a smile. Determined not to show him her pain.

SHEBA

So you're seeing someone else?

*He looks at her, caught. Nods an apology. She stares at him. A stab of
intense jealousy.*

So you just – what – you prefer her? Because she's young?
Huh? Because she helps you with your sums? What –
because she's so nice and tight? I risked my whole life for
you, you little shit!

I never asked you to!

SHEBA

I taught you how to fuck!

Sheba is powerfully conscious she's out of control. She clenches her fists, holds it in, fights back her tears.

STEVEN

Why are you so upset?

She can't answer. He suddenly gets that she loves him. He glances around.

I'd give you a hug but there's people who know me . . . (*Pause.*) I can't deal with this. I'm not old enough.

She's overcome with guilt, tries to be practical.

SHEBA

Steven. Don't be embarrassed at school. Ignore me, OK? You're a sweet boy . . . and I've loved our time together. I'm sorry if I ever harmed you.

He shakes his head.

STEVEN

You never.

They look at each other, tenderly. Then Sheba walks away.

INT./EXT. BARBARA'S CAR/STREET – THAT NIGHT

Barbara driving at speed. Her mood has brightened . . .

She cuts up another car and hurtles along. She spots Sheba outside Steven's estate, a wan figure on the pavement.

Sheba gives her a sad little wave.

Barbara pulls in to the kerb and leaps out. Sheba comes to her, face streaked with tears.

Barbara opens her arms. Forgiveness. They hug. Barbara comforting Sheba – and herself in so doing.

                    BARBARA
                  (*voice-over*)
As Ma would've said, 'The boy done her like a kipper.'

INT. BARBARA'S FLAT – NIGHT

Barbara in her dressing gown, writing her journal.

                    BARBARA
                  (*voice-over*)
She has nowhere to turn but trusty old Ba.

*The silver Asprey frame has pride of place on her mantelpiece. A photo
of Portia inside it.*

INT. SUMMERHOUSE – NIGHT

Sheba wraps the 'S' necklace in paper and puts it in the bin.

                    BARBARA
                  (*voice-over*)
She mopes and mourns for her pubescent paramour – often
at punishing length.

INT. SCHOOL – DAY

*First day of the new term. Barbara watching as Sheba comes in the
main entrance.*

                    BARBARA
                  (*voice-over*)
But she knows my interventions have saved her life and she
is sweetly grateful.

INT. STAFF ROOM – DAY

*Staff buzzing around, comparing their Christmases, moaning about
holidays not being long enough.*

                    BARBARA
                  (*voice-over*)
Her betrayal hurt me more than I dare show.

Barbara sitting in her chair. Sheba comes in. They smile at each other.

But I will forgive her and heal myself in private.

INT. SUMMERHOUSE – NIGHT

Sheba carefully sticking a silver crescent onto Ben's wizard hat.

> BARBARA
> (*voice-over*)
> She's worth it, this one. She's the one I've waited for . . .

INT. LIBRARY, HOMEWORK CLUB – DAY

Barbara patrols the desks.

> BARBARA
> (*voice-over*)
> At last she's beginning to understand that her dalliance
> with Master Connolly was a consequence of her dead
> marriage.

She arrives at Steven's desk. He keeps writing.

INT. RAF MUSEUM – DAY

An outing. Barbara walking with Sheba.

> BARBARA
> (*voice-over*)
> It's a sham – fuelled only by the memory of former glories.

Richard and Ben are behind them, looking at the aeroplanes.

INT. CANTEEN – LUNCHTIME

Sheba and Barbara sitting with their trays, talking.

> BARBARA
> (*voice-over*)
> Whereas we are going through the fire, forging our
> friendship with a stronger bond each day.

INT. CLASSROOM – DAY

Barbara at her high window, watching Sheba lock up her bicycle far below.

> BARBARA
> (*voice-over*)
> In fact, we are now entering a delicate new phase . . .

EXT. ART STUDIO – DAY

Barbara approaches and sees Sheba inside.

> BARBARA
> (*voice-over*)
> We are silently and stealthily negotiating the terms . . . of a life lived together.

Sheba sees Barbara and nods amiably.

INT. SHEBA'S KITCHEN – DAY

Sunday lunch. Barbara at the head of the table, making the family laugh with some anecdote.

> BARBARA
> (*voice-over*)
> Now more than ever we are bound by the secrets we share.

Ben snorts as Barbara makes a funny face.

> BARBARA
> (*voice-over*)
> I'm invited to drop in on them this summer. At their house in the Dordogne. I might just do that . . .

INT. BARBARA'S BEDROOM – NIGHT

Barbara sitting up in bed, writing.

> BARBARA
> (*voice-over*)
> Though no rush. We'll have plenty of time *à deux* once she's left her family . . .

EXT. PARLIAMENT HILL – DAY

Barbara and Sheba on the bench seen at the beginning. They share sandwiches.

> BARBARA
> Do try the prawn, it's delicious.

Barbara munches contentedly.

> I once sat here discussing Elgar. For three hours.

> SHEBA
> God! Who with?

> BARBARA
> Oh, just a friend. Jennifer. This was our haunt.

Sheba conceals her discomfort.

> We were quite chummy for a while. But . . . the poor thing suffered from this terrible depression. I tried to help but she rather unravelled. She became alarmingly . . . deluded.

> SHEBA
> Did she go to hospital?

> BARBARA
> No, she got a job in Stoke.

Sheba thinks, putting it all together . . .

> SHEBA
> When was this?

> BARBARA
> Last summer. I did what I could but she was too far gone. Even so I feel I should've done more . . .

> SHEBA
> I'm sure she knows you did your best . . . you're such a sensitive person.

Sheba pats Barbara's shoulder; Barbara takes her hand.

> BARBARA
> One conceals it of course.

She turns to Sheba, vulnerable.

People languish for years with partners who are clearly from another planet.

SHEBA

Mmm . . .

BARBARA

We so want to believe we've found our 'other'. One needs courage to recognise the real as opposed to the convenient.

SHEBA

Yes.

Barbara is still holding Sheba's hand.

BARBARA

When I was young I had such a vision of myself. I dreamt I'd be someone to be reckoned with. You know, in . . . in the world. (*Beat.*) But one learns one's scale.

Sheba squeezes Barbara's hand. Barbara responds gratefully.

I've such a . . . dread . . . of ending my days alone.

SHEBA

Mmm. Well, we all –

BARBARA

Though, recently, I've allowed myself to imagine I might not be . . . Am I wrong?

SHEBA

Of course not.

Sheba gives Barbara a 'loving' hug. Barbara crumples in gratitude.

EXT. VET'S SURGERY – DAY

Barbara rushes in, cradling the stricken Portia in her arms.

INT. VET'S SURGERY – DAY (LATER)

The Vet feels Portia's tummy.

VET

Do you want to stay?

Barbara shakes her head.

Sometimes people find it comforting to see them at peace.
Would you like to come back . . . in twenty minutes, to say
goodbye?

EXT. STREET – MOMENTS LATER

Barbara comes out of the Vet's. A zombie on the busy street.

*Then she remembers – Sheba lives nearby. She starts to hurry, almost
pushing people out of the way as she rushes to her friend.*

EXT. SHEBA'S STREET – MINUTES LATER

*Barbara panting for breath, a broken woman desperately needing
comfort. She hurries towards Sheba's house.*

*Suddenly – the Harts' car comes out of their driveway nearly knocking
her over. Richard is at the wheel. He parks up, the car skewed on the
road, engine running . . .*

*Ben and Polly are in the back. Barbara sees Polly groaning comically,
mockingly – and Ben (who holds his wizard hat) is laughing at his
sister's antics. Sheba is shushing them.*

*Sheba sees Barbara is in great distress, says something to Richard and
gets out the car.*

Barbara falls into her arms, sobbing.

SHEBA

Is it Portia? Oh no.

*Richard gives Sheba a quizzical look from the car: 'What's up?'
Sheba grimaces, indicates this might take a while.*

Richard exhales in frustration and points to his watch: 'We're late.'

BARBARA

I have to go back to the vet's . . . after it's done . . . Will you
come with me? I just can't on my own . . .

78

SHEBA

Oh, I – of course I would but . . . Ben's doing his play at his school and –

BARBARA

A play?!

SHEBA

The – wizard thing, remember? We're all going. We're a bit late actually . . .

BARBARA

Someone has died!

SHEBA

I – I know . . . and – and it's terribly sad.

Ben is banging on the car window. Richard shouts at Polly to stop him. She shouts back. It's mayhem in there.

BARBARA

You owe me this.

Richard revs the engine, Sheba turns, impossibly pulled in both directions. Richard's face: 'We have to go.'

Ben looks anxiously from the car. Meanwhile, Barbara's on the turn, Sheba pleads:

SHEBA

He's doing a show for the first time in his life!

BARBARA

That's your choice, is it?

SHEBA

Look – why – why don't you come? You're very welcome . . .

Barbara doesn't hear it.

BARBARA

I thought you understood what friendship means.

SHEBA

He's my child!

Richard honks the horn in frustration.

He's my son, he's just a little boy!

BARBARA
Don't play the good mother with me.

Barbara eyes the car – a threat. But now Richard leaps out and shouts across the bonnet.

RICHARD
Excuse me? Can one of you tell me what's going on? Is this some kind of coven?

BARBARA
(*coolly*)
Oh, I can explain perfectly. Would you like me to?

SHEBA
(*interrupting*)
It's just that Barbara's had some very bad news, about her cat.

RICHARD
(*to Barbara*)
My condolences. Poor, poor pussy! Now can I have my wife back please?

BARBARA
(*fixes him*)
I don't like your tone.

RICHARD
(*to Sheba*)
Why is she always here? What fucking spell has she cast on you?!

Polly pokes her head out of the car window.

POLLY
Ben's getting really stressed! I think he's gonna blow!

RICHARD
(*to Sheba*)
God's sake, woman, will you get in the bloody car!

SHEBA

GIVE ME A MINUTE, WILL YOU! I CAN HANDLE
THIS!!

Richard storms back to the car.

BARBARA

Oh – oh – so I'm to be handled, am I? Like toxic waste. So
you see me on sufferance? I'm an imposition, to be tolerated!

Emergency! Sheba hugs Barbara.

SHEBA

No! Of course not! I love our time together! I'm your good,
good friend.

BARBARA

Then stay with me.

SHEBA

I would if I could. And I'm desperately sorry about Portia.
But you know I have to go.

Sheba gently detaches herself. A moment of reckoning:

BARBARA

Think very carefully, madam. Be aware of the consequences.

*The car starts pulling away from the kerb, slowly making its way up
the road.*

SHEBA

Please don't make this mean more than it is!

BARBARA

I need you to stay. I don't know what I'll do . . .

A herculean honk of the horn – and now Sheba runs for it.

SHEBA

I'll phone you later! I promise!

Sheba gets in the car. Barbara watches it disappear down the road.

BARBARA
(*voice-over*)

They always let you down in the end . . .

EXT. BARBARA'S GARDEN – LATER

Barbara digging a hole in the ground with a small trowel.

She's exhausted from the effort, has been sobbing for the last hour. Her hands and arms are covered in soil.

> BARBARA
> (*voice-over*)
> Jennifer said I was 'too intense'. Meaning what exactly?

Barbara buries Portia's body, tightly wrapped in a blanket.

> BARBARA
> (*voice-over*)
> That I am loyal in my friendships?

Then she buries the cat toys and the cat bowl. And with a grim last look – the Asprey frame from Sheba.

> BARBARA
> (*voice-over*)
> That I will go to the ends of the earth for someone I admire?

She treads the earth down.

INT. BEN'S SCHOOL – SAME TIME

Ben's little 'play'. Audience of parents and relatives watching their kids. Richard videos it.

Ben comes on in his wizard hat, waving a wand. Applause and laughter. Sheba is powerfully moved. Polly holds her hand.

INT. BARBARA'S SITTING ROOM – LATE AFTERNOON

It's getting dark outside. Barbara sitting in her chair.

She's still wearing her 'gardening' clothes. Dried mud on her face and arms. She's immobile, a statue in grief.

The door bell rings. She goes down the corridor – hoping it's Sheba come to apologise. She opens the door.

Not disturbing you, am I?

She shakes her head, still dazed by the day's events.

It's just . . . I need to talk to you about Mrs Hart. Sheba.

BARBARA

Ah . . .

She looks at him, feels sure he knows something . . .

BRIAN

It's a bit delicate. Can I come in?

Barbara leads him into the kitchen.

BARBARA

Tea?

BRIAN

Lovely, thanks.

She fetches milk and sugar. Brian hovers.

You haven't got a biscuit?

Barbara produces a tin and hands it to him.

Cheers.

As he munches he notices the muddy trowel on a side table.

BARBARA

Would you like me to take your hat?

He removes his Tottenham Hotspur hat and scarf.

BRIAN

Been up the Lane. White Hart Lane. Home of the mighty Spurs.

BARBARA

Were you victorious?

BRIAN

Three–nil! Jermain Defoe – get in there!

BARBARA

My father supported Charlton Athletic. It never seemed to
give him any pleasure.

Barbara prepares the tea.

BRIAN

Where's the moggy?

BARBARA

She's dead.

Brian eyes the mud on her face and arms.

BRIAN

Oh, dear. My condolences. Ahhh. Is this not a good time?

Barbara thinks. Then, a dark glint in her eye.

BARBARA

It's a very good time.

They sit at the kitchen table.

Mrs Hart.

BRIAN

Yeah. Well . . . it's just . . . erm . . .

BARBARA

Anything you tell me will be in strictest confidence.

He nods, gratefully.

BRIAN

The thing is . . . I was wondering if she's . . . ever
mentioned me?

Barbara's eyes widen.

Does she ever . . . mention me?

BARBARA

Let me think . . .

She puts her fingers to her temples, a little theatrically.

No. Never. (*Beat.*) Actually – yes! She mentioned you'd
invested in a new shirt. I think it was last term.

BRIAN

Yeah, I lashed out at Nicole Farhi. The thing is . . . over the last few months, ever since I met her really, I've . . .

BARBARA

Brian, are you in love?

BRIAN

I've been a bit bloody obvious, haven't I?

BARBARA

You've been utterly clandestine.

He senses she's mocking him but can't be sure.

BRIAN

So she mentioned the shirt, then?

BARBARA

You do know she's married?

BRIAN

Yeah, but she's quite flirty. You never know with people, do you?

BARBARA

Indeed you don't.

BRIAN

But I wouldn't want to make a move if I'm gonna get knocked back. What with staff politics and the Head being such a stickler – you have to be really careful these days.

BARBARA

It's a minefield.

BRIAN

So . . . would . . . do you think you could have a word with her? Suss the lie of the land?

BARBARA

You'd like me to ask Mrs Hart if she's inclined to commit adultery with you?

He looks at her – could not be more exposed. But she's had her fun and is tired of toying with him. To business:

I don't want you to suffer more than is necessary. No one should. I couldn't possibly speak for Mrs Hart but instinct tells me you might not be her type.

Brian nods, crestfallen. Then thinks . . .

BRIAN

She's got a type then?

BARBARA

It's no reflection on your attractiveness. But I get the impression her preference is for . . . the younger man. Surprisingly young. (*Pause.*) Boys, I'm told.

Brian absorbs the information.

Naturally she's never discussed any of this with me. But I've been hearing some rather disturbing rumours that there's one in particular. Playground gossip, staff room whispers and so on . . .

She's alone now, turned away from him, as if he were invisible. Or she in confession.

I think you might know the boy in question . . . Steven Connolly.

BRIAN

Year Ten?

She nods, distantly. Brian stares at her, slow cogs whirring, his moral outrage increasing with his jealousy.

Barbara turns to him now – as if none of this had been said.

BARBARA

I think the kettle's boiled.

INT. BEN'S BEDROOM – THAT NIGHT

Sheba tucking Ben in. His wizard's hat sits on a bedpost. She brushes his hair from his face.

BARBARA
(*voice-over*)

You say the words and it's done. Easy.

86

Sheba kisses Ben goodnight and turns out the light.

INT. BARBARA'S FLAT – SAME TIME

Barbara picking at her dinner in front of the TV, vaguely watching the lottery show.

> BARBARA
> (*voice-over*)
> Judas had the grace to hang himself.

She goes to the kitchen, scrapes her scraps into the bin.

> BARBARA
> (*voice-over*)
> But only according to Matthew – the most sentimental of the apostles.

INT. POLLY'S ROOM – LATER THAT NIGHT

Sheba tidying. She finds a pair of boxer shorts belonging to Polly's boyfriend.

> BARBARA
> (*voice-over*)
> Is this the last night of her old life?

Polly stands in the doorway, having had a bath. Sheba holds up the shorts, quizzically. Polly smiles.

INT. RICHARD'S STUDY – LATER

Richard hard at work. Sheba removes a finished mug of coffee and sets down a new one. He strokes her hand.

> BARBARA
> (*voice-over*)
> I wonder how long my messenger will take?

INT. BATHROOM – NIGHT

Barbara in the bath.

BARBARA

(*voice-over*)

People like Sheba think they know what it is to be lonely.
But of the drip-drip of long-haul, no-end-in-sight solitude
they know nothing.

She draws on her cigarette.

BARBARA

(*voice-over*)

What it's like to construct an entire weekend around a visit
to the launderette. Or to be so chronically untouched that
the accidental brush of a bus conductor's hand sends a jolt
of longing straight to your groin.

INT. SUMMERHOUSE – NIGHT

Sheba alone on the sofa, thinking.

BARBARA

(*voice-over*)

Of this, Sheba and her like have no clue.

INT. BARBARA'S FLAT – SAME TIME

*Barbara in bed. The phone is ringing but she doesn't move. The
ansafone beeps and Sheba leaves her message.*

SHEBA

(*voice-over*)

Ba, I'm so sorry about today. It was an impossible situation.
Richard feels dreadful too. You must be so upset. Poor you.
Poor Portia. Call me as late as you like. Let's not fall out,
come to dinner tomorrow night, OK?

Barbara listens, guilty but resolved.

INT. SITTING ROOM, SHEBA'S HOUSE – EVENING

*Coffee after dinner. Richard lies on a sofa, feet on Sheba's lap. She idly
strokes his calves – not a sight Barbara enjoys as she sits across from
them, nervously smoking.*

RICHARD

Actually, I write quite quickly, it's the thinking that takes an eternity. (*Sighs.*) You're never satisfied; when I'm lecturing I long for time to write and when I've got it I yearn to be back with the students.

From her seat Barbara has a view of the front path. She sees a Woman in her mid-thirties jump out of a car and come storming up to the front door.

Barbara watches Sheba, her last moments before the calamity . . .

SHEBA

More coffee, anyone?

RICHARD

I'll have a slug, please.

SHEBA

Barbara?

BARBARA

No, thank you.

The Woman has now established that the bell makes no sound. She starts to bang on the door. Richard looks at Sheba: 'Who's that?' Sheba shrugs: 'Dunno.'

Richard opens the door. A big Irish voice, full volume:

MRS CONNOLLY

Are you her husband?

RICHARD

What? Whose?

MRS CONNOLLY

Don't you fuck with me, Mister, don't you dick me around! WHERE IS SHE? Tell her Steven Connolly's mother wants to see her right NOW!

Mrs Connolly forces her way in.

RICHARD

Hey, hey, excuse me!

He tries to grab hold of her but she lashes out, catching him across the face. He exclaims in pain.

Sheba comes out into the hall and Mrs Connolly lunges at her, kicking, punching, scratching, screaming.

MRS CONNOLLY

Ya slut! Ya fuckin' whore! How could you! He's only a child! My little boy is a CHILD!

Richard and Barbara manage to pull her off, but she's strong and hurls herself at Sheba again, grasping her hair.

A struggle. Barbara and Richard plant themselves between the two women – keeping them apart in the tight hallway.

RICHARD

What the hell is going on? Will you just stop and calm down for one second, please? PLEASE!

MRS CONNOLLY

You ask your wife what's going on. ASK HER! Ya perverted bitch!

She manages to whack Sheba once more as Mr Connolly appears in the front doorway. A sad, quiet figure.

MR CONNOLLY

Come on. Leave them alone.

He stares at Sheba with contempt.

There's nothing here for us.

He leads his weeping wife down the path back to the car.

Richard closes the front door. Sheba sits at the foot of the stairs, tears streaming.

Richard stares at her, horribly confused . . .

Polly appears at the top of the stairs. Followed by Ben in his pyjamas. Polly's voice, taut with vulnerability:

POLLY

What's happening . . .?

Barbara looks at Sheba, who gives her a weak nod. Barbara climbs the stairs to deal with the children.

INT. LANDING/SITTING ROOM – LATER

Barbara sitting on the stairs with a partial view of the sitting room – where Richard and Sheba are in meltdown.

> BARBARA
> (*voice-over*)
> By the time I took my seat in the gods, the opera was well into its final act . . .

> SHEBA
> It just happened. It just happened!

> RICHARD
> Things don't just – people make them happen. You think you're the only one who's ever wanted someone young? Everyone – sometimes – everyone thinks about it. But they don't act on it, they deal with it!

> SHEBA
> When you met me I was –

> RICHARD
> You were an adult – it's not the same! You're his teacher!

> SHEBA
> And you were mine! I'm not justifying, I'm not saying –

> RICHARD
> Oh, you're so full of shit! It's totally different, you were TWENTY!

> SHEBA
> He'll be sixteen in May! He's not some innocent.

> RICHARD
> Of course he's innocent – he's FUCKING FIFTEEN! Are you INSANE?!

Barbara lights another cigarette – a casual spectator.

If you meant to destroy us, why not do it with an adult?
That's the convention, it's worked for centuries.

                    SHEBA

It wasn't about us.

                    RICHARD

This boy –

                    SHEBA

I told you, it's over.

He holds his head in pain.

                    RICHARD

Why?

                    SHEBA

I . . . just wanted him.

                    RICHARD

Why?

                    SHEBA

I don't know!

                    RICHARD

WELL, FIND OUT!

EXT. SCHOOL – DAY

A police car waits outside the gates.

INT. SCHOOL CORRIDOR – DAY

*Gita with two Police Officers; they head for Pabblem's office. Pupils
pass by, curious.*

INT. STAFF ROOM – DAY

Teachers gossiping as the rumours spread.

INT. SCHOOL CORRIDOR – DAY

Between lessons. Barbara passes Brian as they head in opposite directions.

EXT. SHEBA'S HOUSE – DAY

Two Police Officers walk Sheba to their waiting car. Richard stands in the background.

INT. BARBARA'S BEDROOM – NIGHT

Barbara lies in bed, in the dark.

> BARBARA
> (*voice-over*)
> My guilt is tempered with relief. She assumes the boy cracked and told his mother all. Who am I to disabuse her?

INT. SCHOOL ENTRANCE – DAY

Barbara spots Brian coming in. As he strides away down the corridor:

> BARBARA
> Brian, do stop a moment, please . . .

> BRIAN
> I don't want to hear it.

INT. BARBARA'S FLAT – NIGHT

Barbara watching the news on TV. A report on the 'London teacher sex scandal'.

> TV JOURNALIST
> . . . and there are further unconfirmed reports that a member of staff may have known of the affair . . .

Barbara watches, agog with fear.

INT. PABBLEM'S OFFICE – DAY

The spotless office of a liberal zealot: the pot plants, the good cause posters, a carved 'ethnic' figurine.

> BARBARA
> I've told you, had I known anything I'd have informed you immediately. My only loyalty is to the school!

Pabblem at his desk, doesn't believe a word of it.

> PABBLEM
> Brian thinks you've known for months.

> BARBARA
> Brian 'thinks'?!

> PABBLEM
> And then there's Sue Hodge –

> BARBARA
> Will you be running through the entire staff room?

> PABBLEM
> If you knew and did nothing then you've enabled a crime.

> BARBARA
> I didn't, so I haven't. Your point?

He stares at her, has wanted to do this for years.

> PABBLEM
> I think it would benefit everyone if you retired. With immediate effect.

> BARBARA
> Oh, so it's a witch-hunt – Salem comes to Islington!

She strides to the door but Pabblem gets there first and blocks her exit.

> PABBLEM
> The stress of the job, radical new ideas in teaching not to your taste –

> BARBARA
> I've got an idea: your school, your disaster – why don't you resign?

BECAUSE I AM NOT THE CONFIDANTE OF A
CRIMINAL! Now . . . tell me about this 'friendship' with
Mrs Hart . . .

BARBARA

I think you'll find that a friendship between consenting
adults is perfectly legal – even under your regime. My
record here is beyond reproach, the majority of the staff
regard me as their moral guardian.

*Pabblem quails at the outrageousness of the woman. Barbara tries to
open the door but he stops it, eyeballs her.*

PABBLEM

I've just spoken to another of your 'close' friends. Jennifer
Dodd.

Barbara reacts. He gently closes the door, stares at her, penetrating.

She was most enlightening.

*He has deployed the ultimate weapon. For the first time ever, he's got
her.*

BARBARA

Jennifer became unwell, that's why she left the school.

PABBLEM

She says it's because you were stalking her.

BARBARA

She's an hysteric.

PABBLEM

Jennifer threatened you with an injunction, didn't she?

BARBARA

Nonsense!

He dashes to his desk and brandishes a piece of paper.

PABBLEM

A fax from her solicitors! Jennifer didn't want you within
five hundred yards of her – by law! You call that a
friendship?! She told me you sent her fiancé a wreath!

Barbara looks away, won't let him see her distress.

> Now we wouldn't want all this to come out, would we?
> Thirty years of 'exemplary' service ending in shame and
> humiliation. Hmmm? Your choice, Barbara.

INT. SCHOOL TOILETS – MOMENTS LATER

Barbara vomiting.

Above her head, amongst the graffiti: MAD BABS COVETT — NASTY
OLD LEZZA.

Someone else has scrawled: I WANNA LICK HER MANGY TWAT!!!

INT. STAFF ROOM – LATER

*Tea break. Staff buzz around, agog with the 'Covett sacking rumour'.
Barbara comes in. A pause as people see her.*

*Sue Hodge – big as a barn – stares at her defiantly from Barbara's
own chair. Elaine Clifford serves her tea while other teachers fuss
around her.*

Barbara hurries out of the room.

EXT./INT. BARBARA'S STREET/FLAT – LATE AFTERNOON

Barbara gets out of her car and approaches home. Shattered.

*There's a figure on the other side of the road. He emerges from behind
a car – sees her. They lock eyes. It's Steven. He looks ravaged with
exhaustion and the stress of it all.*

*He comes up to her, close. Barbara bustles past him and he follows,
impassive; it scares her.*

*She rushes down the stairs to her door, fumbling for the key. He follows
after. Just as he comes tearing down the stairs she manages to get in
and slam the door. He bangs at the window in fury.*

*Inside – Barbara clutches herself in fear and shame. Junk mail littered
at her feet.*

She listens . . . relieved to hear the sound of his footsteps up her stone stairs.

> BARBARA
> (*voice-over*)
> He knows. Does she know too? (*Beat.*) More than I can bear.

INT. SITTING ROOM – NIGHT

Barbara in her armchair, curtains drawn. Still and silent.

> BARBARA
> (*voice-over*)
> Is that why she's not returned my calls?

INT. BATHROOM – NIGHT

Barbara removing her make-up. Slow, meticulous, distant. She stares at herself, consumed with self-loathing.

She opens her mirrored cabinet. Tucked in the corner there's a bottle of paracetamol. She focuses on it.

> BARBARA
> (*voice-over*)
> Is this the shape of it? 'Ex-teacher takes life in basement flat.'

And then the phone rings . . .

EXT. SHEBA'S HOUSE – DAY

Press have assembled on the pavement with TV cameras and Photographers – some on stepladders.

Two Police Officers prevent them from storming the front garden.

The Police hold them back as Barbara hurries up the path to the front door, where Richard lets her in.

INT. HALLWAY – CONTINUOUS

Richard looks bedraggled, up-all-night misery. She gestures outside.

BARBARA

Barbarians!

Richard nods. They stand facing each other. A weird echo of their first meeting four months ago.

RICHARD

Sorry about your job.

She's over-emotional and speaks needlessly.

BARBARA

You see, the Headmaster thought I knew!

He's on to her in a flash:

RICHARD

Did you?

BARBARA

No!

They stare at each other.

Where is she?

RICHARD

In her lair.

He gestures outside.

EXT. GARDEN – MOMENTS LATER.

Barbara hurries to the summerhouse. Polly and Sheba are in mid-row. Barbara hides behind a bush.

POLLY

Your boyfriend is younger than mine!

SHEBA

He's not my boyfriend!

POLLY

Don't kid yourself we'll ever forgive you.

SHEBA

I don't expect you to. Hate me – I deserve it. But I won't stop loving you and I won't stop being your mother!

POLLY

The fuck is that?! What's that?! You slept with a child!

Polly storms off, then spots Barbara.

POLLY

Oh, Jesus wept! The spectre at the feast!

BARBARA

Watch your tongue, young lady.

POLLY

Frigging freak!

Barbara knocks on the open door. Sheba turns, relieved to see her. Barbara opens her arms and they hug warmly.

BARBARA

There, there.

Barbara fishes in her bag and gives Sheba a tissue.

Here you are.

Barbara sits Sheba down.

SHEBA

Thanks for coming. (*Pause.*) I'm so sorry about school. Was he awful to you?

Barbara nods, bravely. They sit in silence for a while.

Listen . . . would . . . you can say no . . . I'd completely understand. Richard . . . needs some time alone . . . Actually, he's asked me to leave. Could I come and stay with you? Just for a few days?

Barbara manages to affect the illusion of 'thinking about it' despite her elation.

BARBARA
You're welcome for as long as you like.

Sheba hugs her with gratitude.

INT. HOUSE – LATER

Richard paces in the sitting room as Barbara hovers in the hall.

BARBARA
Is Ben at school?

Richard nods.

Does he . . . know what's happening?

RICHARD
(*furiously*)
It's really none of your business!

Sheba comes down the stairs carrying a suitcase.

Richard gives Barbara a look: 'Go.' Barbara takes the suitcase and goes out of the front door.

Instantly the cameras flash – and then the groans as the Press see it's not who they want.

Richard faces Sheba, his back to the front door.

RICHARD
I knew who you were when we met. You were young. I knew it might get tough. But I was prepared.

He holds her shoulders.

You're a good mother. But at times you've been a fucking lousy wife. Why didn't you come to me? You could've told me how lonely you were. You never trusted me to help you. I'm not saying I'm so fucking fabulous, but I was here.

Sheba accepts it. They look at each other. Then he opens the front door and stands behind it as she goes out.

A huge flash of white light as she faces the cameras.

Fade to:

INT. SITTING ROOM – NIGHT (A MONTH LATER)

                    BARBARA
                  (*voice-over*)
This last month has been the most delicious time of my
life.

*Sheba asleep on the sofa bed. A bare leg exposed. Barbara in an
armchair, watching over her.*

                    BARBARA
                  (*voice-over*)
Of course we've had our ups and downs. The pressure is
intense when two women share their lives.

Her hand hovers over the leg, wants to stroke her but doesn't dare.

                    BARBARA
                  (*voice-over*)
But oh, what marvellous intensity it is!

She carefully covers Sheba's leg with a blanket.

EXT. BARBARA'S FLAT – DAY

A bright Spring day – but the basement curtains are drawn.

*A pack of Journalists, TV Crews and Photographers. They joke
amongst themselves, an atmosphere of crude jollity.*

*The front door opens a crack. They jump into action. Barbara emerges
with her tartan shopping trolley on wheels.*

                 MALE JOURNALIST
    It's the crone!

*Barbara comes up the exterior stairs to ground level. They cluster
around her. Barbara wheels her shopping basket through their midst,
imperious.*

A few give chase but the majority know it's not worth it.

Back at the flat a curtain twitches and the cameras flash.

INT. SITTING ROOM, FLAT

Sheba closes the curtain. She wears a long, ratty T-shirt, knickers and socks.

It's noon. She's just got up. She starts to fold her sheets and blankets. A prisoner.

                    BARBARA
                  (*voice-over*)
          Admittedly, circumstances are not always ideal . . .

INT. BATHROOM

Sheba on the loo, urinating. Utterly desolate.

                    BARBARA
                  (*voice-over*)
          The swinish press, the stringent bail terms, meetings with
          lawyers and so on.

The clutter of Sheba's toiletries and make-up mingled with Barbara's.

                    BARBARA
                  (*voice-over*)
          But all things considered we're coping admirably. In fact,
          gold stars abundant!

Sheba steps on a tiny gold star – incongruously bright and shining – on the grubby floor.

INT. CORRIDOR/BEDROOM – SAME TIME

Sheba comes out the bathroom and wanders down the corridor into Barbara's bedroom.

She hitches up her T-shirt in front of the mirror, broodily posing like an adolescent.

                    BARBARA
                  (*voice-over*)
          The cuckold permits her to see their children once a week.
          Under strict supervision, of course.

Sheba sits at the dressing table. She examines her foot. She picks the gold star off. Odd . . .

> BARBARA
> (*voice-over*)
> There are usually tears – such big, salty tears she cries – and fits of teenage tantrums too.

Sheba puts on some make-up, dark eye-liner, red lips. She's bored out of her brain.

> BARBARA
> (*voice-over*)
> In time she'll recognise she's just not the mothering kind . . .

Sheba stops, spots another gold star on the carpet. She picks it up and flicks it into the bin.

> BARBARA
> (*voice-over*)
> And then Barbara will be there to comfort her: nurse, beloved friend and wise counsel.

The bin is full of cigarette butts, evidence of a long night's work. Sheba sees another gold star amongst the detritus.

> BARBARA
> (*voice-over*)
> I used to waddle through the world virtually invisible, but now I seem somehow to shine.

Sheba spots a scrap of crumpled paper ripped from a notebook – two gold stars on it.

> BARBARA
> (*voice-over*)
> At last, I am me.

Sheba takes the scrap of paper from the bin. Sees Barbara's handwriting on it. Sheba reads . . .

Close: the page from Barbara's journal.

Sheba reading in horror.

INT. SUPERMARKET — SAME TIME

Barbara choosing food, comparing prices — has to be frugal.

She merrily picks out a big, white loaf. Fish fingers, sausages, baked beans. Comfort food.

INT. BARBARA'S BEDROOM

Sheba leaps up, pulls open a dressing-table drawer: make-up. Another: a hair dryer. Another: stationery; pens, paper and a packet of gold stars . . .

Sheba frantically searches, ransacking the place.

INT. SUPERMARKET — SAME TIME

Barbara queues at the checkout, chatting with her fellow shoppers. No longer one of the lonely — a woman of purpose.

INT. BARBARA'S BEDROOM

Sheba searches drawers, under the bed, in cupboards, turns out the laundry basket — until finally . . . in the bottom of a little drawer beneath the mirror, she finds the journal.

She flicks through: Barbara's black ink handwriting — mainly neat, but now and then with violent crossings out and furious, mad, margin scrawlings.

The gold stars charting the various ups and downs . . .

A photo: Barbara and Jennifer Dodd in Paris, smiling at the camera. Jennifer is around the same age as Sheba, a similar look.

Beneath the photo Barbara has written, 'Paris 2003 — before the worm turned.'

On another page Sheba finds a Pizza Express receipt marked 'Ladies who lunch!!!'

And there are numerous clippings from recent newspaper reports on the scandal.

On an earlier page a strand of hair is taped in. Barbara's handwriting:
'A strand of her hair.'

Sheba reads on with mounting horror . . .

EXT. STREET/BARBARA'S FLAT – LATER

Barbara wheeling her full shopping trolley down the street. The Press
still camped outside her flat.

> JOURNALIST
> The crone returneth!

Barbara sails through the hordes.

INT. BARBARA'S FLAT – CONTINUOUS

She lets herself in. Instantly knows something's wrong.

> BARBARA
> Sheba . . . ?

The flat has been completely trashed. Furniture and cushions ripped
with a carving knife, crockery smashed, books and ornaments torn
from shelves.

Sheba is sitting on the edge of an armchair. Fully dressed now,
wearing her coat, her suitcase by her side.

She's savage with rage – clutching the journal. Her make-up
disturbing, eyes black with mascara, lips a violent red.

> SHEBA
> What you say, about me, about Richard. You're not fit to
> shine his shoes. And Ben and Polly . . . that I'd be better off
> without them?

Sheba rises. Slowly approaches. Barbara holds her ground.

> Why did you do it? Because I didn't help you collect your
> CAT?!

Sheba slaps her hard across the face. Barbara flinches but doesn't
budge, accepting her punishment.

Sheba slaps her again. Barbara stands firm, taking it, despite the pain.

BARBARA

Let it all out . . .

SHEBA

You've cost me my family!

BARBARA

Oh, take some responsibility! They'd have found out in the end! I've given you exactly what you wanted – without me you'd still be stuck in that marriage!

SHEBA

What?!

BARBARA

You can't accept it yet but –

SHEBA

You think I wanted to be HERE WITH YOU!!

BARBARA

Maybe you didn't want it to – to happen quite like this, but we both know you need me, I'm your friend!

SHEBA

You've put me in prison, I could get TWO YEARS!

BARBARA

They'll fly by! I'll visit every week. We have so much life to live – together!

SHEBA

You – WHAT? You think this is a LOVE affair?! A relationship?!

She brandishes the journal as evidence.

Sticky gold stars and – and – a strand of my HAIR?! A receipt from PIZZA EXPRESS?! (*Gestures to the room.*) It's a basement flat off the ARCHWAY ROAD and you think you're Virginia frigging Woolf! And where did you get my hair? Did you pluck it from the bath with some special fucking tweezers?!

BARBARA

Don't you know it's rude to read a person's diary, it's
PRIVATE!

Barbara lunges for the diary but Sheba pulls it away.

SHEBA

It's all BULLSHIT! We're not COMPANIONS, we're not
FRIENDS – you don't even like me!

BARBARA
(*urgently*)
No! I – I have only tender feelings for you – only love!

SHEBA

YOU'RE BARKING FUCKING MAD! You don't know
how to LOVE! You've never – your whole life – me – Jennifer
fucking Dodd – you're just WASTE and disappointment,
you DYKE, you BITTER OLD VIRGIN! Endlessly
justifying yourself with how lonely you are – you're lonely
for a REASON! They hated you at school – all of them –
for THIRTY YEARS! I was the idiot who bothered, but
only 'cos no one told me you're a VAMPIRE! So what is it,
Ba – you – you wanna roll around on the floor like *lovers*?!
You wanna fuck me, Barbara?

BARBARA

Please don't diminish our –

SHEBA

Our *what*?! Our WHAT?!

*Sheba starts ripping out the sacred pages from the diary. Barbara
fights for the book, desperate to rescue it.*

BARBARA

Give it back!

They tug and pull – struggling – locked together.

I know you – born selfish and vain – think you've a divine
right – you BIG BABY! You don't belong in the world,
YOU BELONG HERE!

Sheba lets out a roar of fury right in Barbara's face.

SHEBA

AAAAAAAGGGGGHHHHH!!!

Barbara releases her grip and Sheba tears the book from her. She runs out of the front door – wild.

EXT. STREET – CONTINUOUS

Sheba charges up the basement steps only for the amazed Press to surround her.

SHEBA

HERE I AM! HERE I AM!

Sheba screams and howls, giving them exactly what they want. Barbara watches it all from her window.

JOURNALIST 1

Oh my God, she's gone berserk!

JOURNALIST 2

It's Christmas!

Sheba tries to break through them but is trapped in their tight circle. She's scared now . . .

SHEBA

Please . . . let me go now . . . that's enough . . . please . . .

They continue to flash their cameras and pummel her with questions.

Barbara rushes out of the door and barges through them, elbowing her way with all the force in her body – a strangely heroic little figure amongst the seething men.

BARBARA

Let me through you OAF – GET OUT MY WAY – Give us some room here!

She manages to hustle an almost grateful Sheba back into the flat. She slams the door.

INT. HALLWAY – CONTINUOUS

Barbara and Sheba getting their breath. Two fighters all punched out.

INT. BARBARA'S FLAT – LATER THAT NIGHT

Barbara with a big, black bin-liner tidying the mess. She scoops some broken glass into the bag.

Sheba at the kitchen table, still holding the journal.

> SHEBA
> We never invited you to the fucking Dordogne.

> BARBARA
> I'm sorry, but you specifically said if I happened to be in France then I must drop –

> SHEBA
> We didn't mean it!

Barbara forces herself to stay calm.

> BARBARA
> Well . . . fine. (*An afterthought.*) I won't come then.

Sheba shakes her head: 'Bonkers.' She puts on her coat.

> SHEBA
> I asked you to lunch because I liked you. I would've been your friend.

> BARBARA
> (*softly*)
> I need more than a friend.

They look at each other. No anger, just stalemate. Sheba hands Barbara the journal and leaves.

Barbara in her trashed flat. Desolate.

She places the journal on an empty shelf.

INT./EXT. TAXI/LONDON STREETS – LATER

Sheba in a cab, heading home.

EXT. SHEBA'S HOUSE – NIGHT

Sheba standing outside her house. Warm lights on inside.

She climbs the stairs and nervously knocks on the door.

After a while Richard opens it. They look at each other.

And then he motions her in and closes the door.

EXT. HIGH STREET – DAY (A WEEK LATER)

Bustle of people. Barbara amongst them.

INT. STATIONER'S

Barbara selects a new journal from the shelf.

She goes to the checkout – ignoring the section where they sell the gold stars.

EXT. BARBARA'S STREET

Barbara walking, her new journal in its plastic bag. She heads down the concrete stairs to her front door.

INT. BARBARA'S FLAT, SITTING ROOM – DAY

Barbara at her kitchen table. The flat looks bare and bleak, stripped of all life.

She takes out her new diary and smooths down the spine on the first page.

She uncaps her pen, poised to write.

She thinks. Nothing to say.

She sits in silence.

EXT. PARLIAMENT HILL – DAY (THREE MONTHS LATER)

Close on newspaper headline: SEX TEACHER SENTENCED TO TEN MONTHS.

Under it a press photo of Sheba being shepherded into court by Richard.

A Woman is sitting on 'the' bench, reading the newspaper. She sips a takeaway cappuccino, reads on, engrossed in the story.

> BARBARA
> (*out of shot*)

I knew her . . .

The Woman turns, Barbara is standing behind her.

> WOMAN

Really?

> BARBARA

We taught at the same school.

> WOMAN

God. What was she like?

> BARBARA
> (*thinks*)

. . . A bit chilly. And perhaps a touch . . . furtive. A sort of absent person. But I didn't know her well. (*Beat.*) May I?

She sits next to the Woman.

> WOMAN

Do you still teach?

> BARBARA

No, no, retired. Thank goodness.

The Woman sips her coffee, producing a little dab of froth on her nose. Barbara points to it, amused. The Woman shrugs, charmingly, and searches for a tissue. In an instant Barbara produces one and hands it to her.

> WOMAN

Thanks.

They sit back admiring the view.

> BARBARA

I do love it here.

WOMAN

Mmm.

BARBARA

It's spectacular at dusk.

Barbara turns to her lovely new prey.

I'm Barbara.

WOMAN

Annabel.

They shake hands.

As they continue to talk, the camera moves behind them to take in the view, as at the beginning.

Two women on a bench. The city in the distance.

Fade to black.